Esly Carvalho, with Bianca Bassi

Brainspotting
Sessions

Where You Look Affects How You Feel

TraumaClinic
Edições

©2025 Esly Regina Carvalho
All rights reserved.

Author: Esly Carvalho
Editor: Bianca Breus Bassi
Publisher: TraumaClinic Edições
Translator: Esly Carvalho
Cover Art: Esly Carvalho
Cover Design: Ederson Luciano Santos de Oliveira
Typesetting/Layout: Manoel Menezes

Library of Congress Cataloging-in-Publication Data

Carvalho, Esly; Bassi, Bianca B.

Brainspotting sessions: where you look affects how you feel / Esly Carvalho and Bianca Breus Bassi. – First edition.

228 p. cm.

"Original title: Relatos de sessões de Brainspotting: Como onde você olha afeta o que você sente."

Includes bibliographical references.

ISBN 978-1-968119-07-2 (pbk.)

1. Brainspotting (Psychotherapy) — Case studies.

2. Trauma — Treatment.

3. Psychotherapy — Methodology.

[Library of Congress Control Number to be assigned]

TraumaClinic Edições — www.traumaclinic.com.br

TraumaClinic
Edições

"Where you look affects how you feel"

David Grand

Special thanks...

To David, who has always recognized and admired my pioneering spirit. Gratitude is an eternal emotion and never dies. Here's our first Brainspotting casebook.

To my parents, (Zilda and Loamy) my grandmother (Vó Mindinha) all of blessed memory, and my aunt-godmother, (Dindinha) who early on saw the talent I did not see nor perceive in myself, yet sacrificed their immigrant income so that I could pursue some initial art studies. You gave me the genes to do it.

I am glad that God has given us life and health for my aunt to live to see my work.

Special gratitude to Bianca, whose amazing editorial gift transformed videos into written art. This would not have been so beautiful, clear and moving without your time and investment in this project. I hope it will be the first of many.

To all of the amazing people who shared their stories with me, with us, and let their blessing extend to you, the reader. Thank you for your generosity.

And to those who tread the pathways of these stories, may they touch you with the healing power of Brainspotting as it has me.

Esly Carvalho

Table of Contents

Part 4 – Brainspotting Sessions Z-Axis

Part 5 – Brainspotting Sessions Z-Axis with the Resource Eye

Presentation

I didn't discover Brainspotting, I noticed it. When the champion ice skater, blocked in her ability to complete a triple loop, manifested a powerful eye wobble and freeze while tracking my fingers, I stopped in place with a reflexive startle response. I had no idea that over two decades later I would have shepherded a healing modality around the globe. It was also no mistake that the noticing happened with a performance block because Brainspotting is so intertwined with performance and creativity.

A few years later I was holding the same healing frame with a blocked Brazilian painter, who happened to be a therapist and trainer as well. I can still see Esly Carvalho sitting across from me gazing at the tip of a pointer I was strategically holding in place. She reflected it had been twenty years since she had painted last and she desperately wanted to grasp and fluidly move her brush again. It was a tall task indeed but I had complete faith in both of us in our joint (ad)venture. In the weeks, months and years to come I was blessed to see the fruit of our two hour healing journey. Vibrant colors, dynamic movement; soul expressed and revealed on canvas.

Since then, Esly has helped me not only spread Brainspotting healing around Brazil, but we have also pioneered to Portugal, Spain and Latin America.

Every reader can easily identify with the artists and their stories. I can as well as I discovered in my forties that my art form is creative writing, and I am proud to be an artist in the global community of artists.

This book tells not only this story, but, looking backward and forward at the double helix of healing and creativity, the harmonic symphony of artists of all stripes exploring their paths of creative rebirth, expression and healing, we will meet others who have also encountered the healing power of Brainspotting. Here you will find stories of suffering and redemption, tears and tenderness, and the vulnerable courage to heal.

David Grand, 2025

Preface

"It's been 20 years since I've picked up a paintbrush."

David looked at me with interest and compassion. He knew very well what that meant for an artist.

"So, is that what you want to work on?"

"Yes. I want my creativity back, my paintbrushes, the strong colors, to be able to express my soul on paper again."

David invited me to a Brainspotting session when he was just beginning to develop his new way of working. Two hours later, I left certain that I would return to painting.

I did. Not only did I return to painting, but I also had the piano tuned and bought a guitar again. And I resumed painting, but this time for good, embracing myself as an artist. For this reason, the cover of this book is my "chapter" of the story: proof that Brainspotting opens and heals places within us that cause our creativity and capacity for expression to blossom. I am still painting today, and more and more.

In the following pages, you will also find my creative ways of interweaving and dialoguing with patients. As many know, my initial training was in Psychodrama, an excellent marriage with Brainspotting. You will see the influence of my psychodramatic training, which continues to be my great professional passion. Here you can see that the theoretical framework, above all, is the repair of the ruptures that life brings us. Hemingway said that "life breaks us all, but some become strong in our broken places." Painting continues to strengthen the places that broke within me, as does future expectations.

This collection of sessions took place over several different Brainspotting modules between 2020 and 2023. In some of my groups, there were many participants of Christian faith, hence the religious mention at various points, always with the utmost ethical respect, as any psychotherapy demands. In several sessions, various situations unfolded. Sometimes it's hard not to get lost in this chronology, but I always try to stitch together as many experiences as possible that are on the same thread of memories. This way, the person comes out not only cut open, but also well-sutured.

I hope that my Brainspotting colleagues can benefit from the experiences offered here in this book. And for the many people seeking healing for their hearts, perhaps they can find part of that in these accounts and in this approach that has blessed so many.

Esly Carvalho, Ph.D., T.E.P
Brasília, July 2025.

Introduction

Since David Grand discovered Brainspotting (BSP) in 2003, the technique has been spreading rapidly across the world. Born out of clinical practice and the attentive listening to the body's signals, this intraexperimental approach quickly attracted psychotherapists seeking deep and effective interventions for the treatment of trauma, physical and emotional pain, anxiety, phobias, creative blocks, and many other challenges.

Today, more than 20,000 professionals have been trained in Brainspotting across 52 countries, spanning every major continent. In Brazil, the technique has been growing exponentially, with training programs that follow international standards and an active community of therapists who support each other in both practice and theoretical development.

Although still relatively recent, the literature on Brainspotting already includes key works in several languages. Among the most relevant titles are:

- *Brainspotting: The Revolutionary New Therapy for Rapid and Effective Change* — David Grand (2013), the foundational work, translated into several languages, including Portuguese;

- *The Power of Brainspotting: An International Anthology* — Gerhard Wolfrum (2018), a collection of international cases and perspectives;

- *Brainspotting with Young People: An Adventure into the Mind* — Mark Grixti (2015), focused on working with children and adolescents;

- *Healing Trauma with Brainspotting* — Christian Zaczyk (2019), a French-language publication that expands the clinical discussion of the technique;

• And other works such as *This Is Your Brain on Sports* by David Grand, and *Brainspotting with Children and Adolescents* by Monika Baumann.

These titles highlight applications of the method in diverse contexts: from treating complex trauma to enhancing athletic and artistic performance, from clinical work with children to interventions with groups and at-risk populations. Yet, despite this growing body of literature, one significant gap remains: very few books provide real session transcripts that allow readers to see, in practice, how Brainspotting unfolds in the therapeutic setting.

This book was created with that very purpose: to offer a collection of real sessions, transcribed with care, sensitivity, and an unwavering commitment to patient confidentiality. Names, places, and other identifying details have been changed to preserve privacy, without compromising the emotional and clinical integrity of each person's process. Readers will find here accounts of sessions using different Brainspotting configurations — including activation and resource spots, the Z-axis, the outside window, among others — always grounded in authentic experiences from the therapy room.

This book is written to inspire curious readers interested in psychology, as well as fellow psychologists — whether already trained in Brainspotting and seeking deeper understanding, or new to the method and looking for a solid overview of its applications. By sharing these stories, we hope to provide material that is thoughtful, practical, and reflective: inspiring trained psychologists to deepen their expertise or seek certification to integrate Brainspotting into their clinical practice with confidence; and encouraging curious readers to seek out a trained therapist to address their own issues in a profound and transformative way.

Chapter 1

The Origin of Brainspotting and Its Evolution

Brainspotting (BSP) was discovered in 2003 by American psychotherapist David Grand, PhD, while working with a high performance ice-skater using EMDR (Eye Movement Desensitization and Reprocessing). During the session, Grand noticed that the client displayed an unusual response when her gaze fixed on a specific point in space. By keeping her eyes on that spot, he observed that an intense neurophysiological processing began—deeper and more spontaneous than what had been happening with standardized EMDR protocols. This clinical moment gave rise to what he would later name Brainspotting.

David Grand was already well known for his work with athletes, artists, and survivors of complex trauma. Initially trained in EMDR, he had also studied extensively *Somatic Experiencing (SE)*, Ericksonian hypnosis, and other "mind-body" approaches. Despite these previous influences, Brainspotting emerged as an original method with its own identity. Since then, the technique has been continuously developed and refined, grounded in clinical observation, applied neuroscience, and feedback from hundreds of therapists around the world.

The phrase that became something of a guiding principle of the method—*"Where you look affects how you feel"*—captures the essence of

BSP. The central idea is that certain eye positions directly access neural networks linked to the client's emotional and somatic experience. When the brain is stimulated through these "spots" (neuropsychological access points located via the visual field), it activates a process of self-regulation and deep reprocessing. These points are identified through reflexive bodily responses—such as blinking, swallowing, involuntary movements, or changes in breathing—that the therapist observes while the client is in a state of emotional activation.

"That certain eye positions directly access neural networks linked to the client's emotional and somatic experience. When the brain is stimulated through these "spots" (neuropsychological access points located via the visual field), it activates a process of self-regulation and deep reprocessing."

Brainspotting has established itself as a relational approach. Rather than interpreting, the therapist acts primarily as a *facilitator*: a witness and participant in the process, holding space for the client's system to reorganize based on its own inherent capacity.

Since its initial discovery, different configurations and branches of the method have emerged, expanding its range of clinical applications. Among the most notable are:

- **Activation Spot and Resource Spot**: strategies that use the difference in activation or resource points in the eyes to either intensify or soften the emotional experience, depending on the client's needs.

- **Outside Window and Inside Window**: approaches in which the therapist either identifies reflexive responses in the client (outside window) or the client detects their own sensitive points (inside window).

- **Z-Axis**: a three-dimensional variation of BSP, in which the distance between the pointer and the client's eyes, or the focal point of vision, is used as a therapeutic factor.

• **Gazespotting, Rolling Spotting**, and other modalities that allow for more flexible and specific adaptations, depending on the client's profile and the clinical situation.

Here are the explanations for these techniques in greater detail.

Activation Spot and Resource Spot

In Brainspotting, the eyes are not merely instruments for receiving visual stimuli, but "portals" to the inner world. The direction of a person's gaze can activate, modulate, or even soften deep emotional experiences. Among the most commonly used strategies for this are the concepts of the Activation Spot and the Resource Spot.

Activation Spot

The Activation Spot is the eye position that connects the client directly to the content that needs to be processed. By fixing their gaze to a particular point within the visual field, the client experiences an increase in emotional, bodily, or cognitive activation associated with the issue at hand—whether it is a specific memory, a diffuse feeling, or a physical state of discomfort. The therapist observes reflexive signals that indicate this sensitivity: micro-movements, swallowing, subtle tremors, changes in facial expression, pupil dilation, among others.

This visual "spot" functions as an "entryway" into specific neural networks. By maintaining the gaze there, the client allows the brain to access implicit material often beyond the reach of verbal narrative. Processing takes place at a deep, self-regulating, nonlinear—and often surprising—level.

Resource Spot

The Resource Spot, on the other hand, is intended to provide emotional support and safety for the client's system. When a client finds this spot, they will often experience relief, stability, or a sense of inner strength. It can be used at the beginning of a session to create a secure foundation, during the process to offer regulation in moments of heightened activation, or even as the primary focus of work in more delicate cases.

In some sessions, the therapist may alternate between both eyes—for example, activating a more sensitive spot and then returning to the Resource Spot to help the system integrate or reorganize. This respects the client's internal rhythm and allows greater flexibility in clinical practice.

It is important to emphasize that both the Activation Spot and the Resource Spot can be found either by observing bodily reactions (in the Outside Window) or by following the client's subjective perception (in the Inside Window). What matters, more than verbal logic, is the somatic response: the body speaks, and the therapist observes with a trained eye.

Outside Window and Inside Window

In Brainspotting, the term *window* refers to the way in which the therapist and client access activation or resource spots within the visual field. The two primary modalities are called the Outside Window and the Inside Window. Both aim to locate brainspots, but they follow different paths—one guided by the therapist's observation, the other by the client's subjective awareness.

Outside Window

In the Outside Window, the therapist guides the search for the visual spot based on the reflexive signals observed in the client. These are involuntary bodily responses that occur as the pointer (or the therapist's finger) is moved slowly across the visual field. Common signs include blinking, swallowing, sudden changes in breathing, microexpressions, subtle tremors, or shifts in skin tone.

These signals indicate that the brain is accessing relevant material—often implicit or not yet verbalized—when looking in that direction. The therapist then "freezes" the pointer at that spot and invites the client to maintain their gaze there, allowing the neurophysiological processing to unfold.

This window is particularly useful in cases where clients struggle to identify internal sensations, are highly dissociated, or tend to over-rationalize their experiences. The Outside Window offers a kind of "shortcut" through the body, trusting the wisdom of the nervous system to point the way.

Inside Window

In the Inside Window, it is the client who guides the search for the brainspot. The therapist uses a pointer and invites them to look slowly across their visual field and notice, with mindful attention, where they feel the strongest activation, discomfort, tension, emotion, or any other significant sensation related to the issue being worked on.

When the client identifies the point of greatest intensity (or, in some cases, the point of greatest resource), they indicate it, and processing begins there.

The Inside Window is especially effective when clients have good self-awareness, can easily identify physical and emotional shifts, and feel comfortable engaging in this type of self-observation. It also promotes client autonomy and a more active role in the therapeutic process.

These two windows are not mutually exclusive—many sessions combine both approaches. There are also complementary variations, such as the *Intuitive Window*, in which the client simply points to a spot that "feels right," without necessarily knowing why, which can later be confirmed or refined with the therapist's guidance.

Z-Axis

The Z-Axis represents an additional dimension within Brainspotting, expanding the ways in which the visual field can be used as a therapeutic tool. While activation and resource spots are identified based on the horizontal and vertical directions of gaze (the X and Y axes), the Z-Axis refers to the depth of the visual field—the distance between the focal point and the client's eyes.

This technique was developed by David Grand after noticing that moving the pointer (or a finger, or any other visual target) closer to or farther from the client's eyes could intensify, soften, or transform the emotional experience associated with the brainspot. From this, the idea emerged that each person has an "optimal processing zone," which can vary from session to session—or even within the same session, depending on the material accessed.

Working with the Z-Axis is particularly useful when clients have difficulty accessing emotional material, when there is freezing or dissociation, or when the goal is to deepen an already-identified spot to reach more subtle layers of processing. This approach also allows for more direct respect of the client's system, offering modulation options without needing to change the visual point horizontally or vertically.

In practice, the therapist slowly moves the pointer closer or farther away while the client keeps their gaze fixed in the original direction. During this movement, the therapist observes whether there are changes in bodily signals or in the client's subjective perception. Often, even a small adjustment in distance can unlock processing or bring forth a new wave of integration.

Rolling Spotting

Rolling Spotting is a dynamic technique that facilitates access to activation points in cases of blockage, emotional overload, or when the client has difficulty focusing on a specific spot. The client is invited to gently move their eyes from side to side while keeping the activated theme in mind. During this continuous movement, the therapist observes whether there is a point at which emotional or bodily activation intensifies—and if so, that spot can then be fixed for processing (Ross & Cohen, 2017).

This technique can be carried out with or without a pointer and is considered a variation of the Outside Window model. Its use is acknowledged in advanced Brainspotting trainings and is described as a versatile clinical resource for making the start of the therapeutic process more flexible.

Gazespotting

Gazespotting is one of the most spontaneous and "organic" forms of Brainspotting. In this approach, the therapist observes where the client's eyes naturally drift while they are speaking about an emotionally charged issue. Typically, at some point, the gaze becomes involuntarily fixed in a particular direction—and that spot is then maintained as the focus for processing.

In this case, the client's gaze itself becomes an emotional compass. The therapist may mirror the eye position or simply acknowledge the intuitively discovered brainspot. No pointer or specific instructions are required. The focus is on following the wisdom of the client's system and respecting its spontaneity.

This technique is often used with clients who are already familiar with the therapeutic process or when the therapeutic relationship is well established. It can be extremely gentle, deep, and effective—precisely because it trusts what emerges naturally.

Summary

Brainspotting is a therapeutic approach rich in possibilities, with different configurations that allow the therapist to adapt the work to the needs of each client, moment, and theme. Among its main variations are:

- **Activation Spot**: focuses on the visual point that intensifies the emotional or somatic experience, facilitating access to material that needs processing.

- **Resource Spot**: focuses on a visual point that offers safety, stability, or inner strength, serving as an anchor in moments of greater activation.

- **Outside Window**: the therapist observes the client's bodily reflexes to locate the brainspot.

- **Inside Window**: the client identifies, based on their subjective perception, the most significant visual point.

- **Rolling Spotting**: the eyes move gently from side to side until a point of greater activation spontaneously emerges.

- **Gazespotting**: the therapist observes the natural direction of the client's gaze while they speak, identifying the brainspot intuitively and spontaneously.

- **Z-Axis**: adjusts the depth of the pointer (closer to or farther from the eyes) to find the optimal processing zone.

- **One-Eye Brainspotting**: when the client covers one eye to find the resource eye and the activation eye. Special glasses may be used for this purpose—one lens transparent and the other opaque—allowing the therapist to alternate or maintain the use of the glasses throughout the session.

These modalities are not mutually exclusive—they often intertwine within a single session or throughout the therapeutic process. The therapist's role is to be familiar with these tools and apply them ethically, responsively, and in attunement with the unique moment of each client.

In the following pages, we will explore these configurations in greater depth, contextualizing their use in the transcribed sessions that make up this book.

The Clinical Use of Brainspotting and the Therapist's Stance

Brainspotting is not only a technique for neurophysiological access, but also a deeply relational approach. Its practice requires a kind of listening that goes beyond words—listening to the body, to silence, and to the subtle signals of presence and activation.

Unlike more directive models, BSP invites the therapist to adopt a stance of compassionate neurobiological witnessing. This means holding a safe, regulated, and nonjudgmental space where the client's system can reorganize itself. Trust in the wisdom of the brain and body is central to this process.

In clinical practice, this translates into:

Full presence: the therapist shows up as whole, regulated, and attentive not only to what the client says, but also to how their system responds.

- **Observation without interference**: there is a commitment to non-direction, especially at the beginning of the process. The therapist accompanies but does not interfere with the content or the course of processing.
- **Mutual regulation**: the therapeutic bond functions as a system of co-regulation, in which the therapist's stability provides a safe model for the client.
- **Permission for the nonverbal**: in Brainspotting, silence can be therapeutic. Many sessions unfold with little dialogue but with intense internal movements.
- **Technical flexibility**: the therapist chooses the most suitable modality (Outside Window, Inside Window, Rolling, etc.), yet remains available to adjust the path according to what emerges in the session.

To the Reader

In the following pages, you will find clinical accounts based on real Brainspotting sessions, carefully transcribed and adapted for fluent reading without compromising the integrity of the therapeutic process. Each case was selected for bringing distinct elements of the method— different configurations, life stories, and ways in which the nervous system responds to the deep work with brainspots.

Names, locations, and any identifiable data have been modified to preserve client confidentiality, in accordance with the ethical principles of psychological practice. However, the emotional content, inner movements, and lived experiences have been faithfully preserved, honoring the subjective truth of each journey.

We invite you to read not only with an analytical mind, but also with an open heart. As you follow these sessions, allow yourself to feel alongside them, notice the details, reflect on your own clinical work, and perhaps rediscover the beauty that inhabits the therapeutic space when healing happens from the inside out.

Part 1

Brainspotting Sessions with the Outside Window

Chapter 2

Amanda Hands Over the Keys

D uring one of the online Brainspotting training classes, Amanda, one of the participants, shared that she had suffered from headaches since childhood. In adulthood, she was diagnosed with migraines. Although she said that at that point the pain was more manageable, it still caused considerable distress.

The session began with the therapist moving the pointer while Amanda followed it with her eyes. Gradually, activation points were identified. When Amanda fixed her gaze on one of them, she reported a moderate activation, around 5 (on a scale from 0 to 10), and a sensation localized in her chest. From that moment until the end of the session, Amanda maintained her focus on that spot.

When invited to reflect on the origin of her migraines, Amanda acknowledged that her crises were often linked to the anticipation of events—whether positive or challenging. She recalled a specific episode during an EMDR course in Brasília, when she arrived with an intense headache, fearing she would not be able to participate. At that time, she remembered a question posed by the therapist: *"How old is the little girl who's there?"* The immediate answer that always came to her was *"eight years old."*

— I remember that as a child, whenever I had a headache, my stomach would get upset and I'd end up vomiting. That's why I feel the two were connected. But when I got older, it seemed that link between stomach and headache no longer existed, unless the migraine was extremely severe—then I would still feel nauseous. But I've noticed that both good things and challenging things, whenever they're about to happen, can trigger a migraine at times.

— And that eight-year-old girl, tell me a little about her, said the therapist.

— Well, what always comes to mind at eight years of age is that I had surgery to remove my tonsils. I was in second grade, I remember my teacher, but I don't really recall much else.

— What was that like? What did they tell you? Did anything happen that you remember specifically?

— My mother told me that ever since I was born, I had constant throat problems, one infection after another. I was on antibiotics all throughout my childhood, and I always had fevers. She used to say sometimes the fever was so high I would start to get delirious. She couldn't take it anymore and finally took me to the doctor, who recommended surgery. From birth until age eight I suffered with tonsillitis. After my tonsils were removed, I never had any more problems — not even pharyngitis, nothing. Sometimes, when I feel a migraine coming, I sense something rising here, in my nose. But the migraine itself is usually either on the left or right side.

— So, it seems you never had those childhood complications again, but, on the other hand, you got the headache.

— Yes, it seems like it came to replace them. My hands are cold right now, they're shaking.

— Amanda spoke with a slightly choked voice.

— Were there any complications during that surgery?

— No, none. In fact, I remember some good things afterward, like being given ice cream because I had to take cold things. I also received a gift from my aunt after the surgery, so there were good moments.

— Did they explain what they were going to do?

— Not that I remember. The feeling I have is that something... something remained open.

— Well, then do your internal scan, look inside—what is open in there? — the therapist asked.

— I don't know, the emotion... But it feels like... it feels like I had to swallow everything. And since I was a very "good" child, I accepted everything without complaining, because there were expectations of me. It was as if I always had to set an example; I am the oldest, the only daughter, which is why I always tried to be the best student.

Gradually, the session began to reach deeper layers. Amanda recalled an old therapy exercise in which she had drawn various "weights" around herself. The therapist asked:

— If these weights could speak, what would they say?

— "You can't disappoint others," "You can't be angry." Amanda responded firmly. — That's really how I feel when I have a migraine. It's a kind of exhaustion, a discouragement. Just thinking about it makes me feel discouraged too, like I want to stay in my corner and disappear. Many times, I wanted to sleep just so I wasn't there; for me, sometimes sleeping was really an escape, an escape from something.

— Exactly, you have to be perfect. Looks like you still feel you have to be perfect, right?

The connection between physical symptoms and emotional states began to emerge more clearly.

— I've always said that my mother's last name is guilt, and it seems I feel a lot of guilt when I think about things I didn't do, or I think I didn't do well, with my children—and these "weights" come up. When I realize something isn't going well for them, it feels like I have to do something to fix it, but I can't always do that... and that has turned into a control issue for me. It's very difficult for me to have to control everything.

— Yes, because control is, in fact, an illusion; nobody really has it. Since when do we control children? Control a husband, control a wife? That doesn't exist, said the therapist.

— When I see them going through some difficulty, it feels like I have to solve it, like it's my responsibility to do something. And when I feel that with my children or something else, my heart races, I get a stomachache... Amanda placed her hand on her stomach, with an expression of pain, while keeping her eyes on the brainspot.

— And how does all of this help you?

— It's because it seems like only recently have I started connecting all these things, and it feels like I'm trying to put everything together to see if I can understand it.

— Do you need to understand in order to heal?

— I don't know.

Amanda responded with a smile, trying to connect her feelings with the emerging insights about herself. The therapist continued deepening the reprocessing:

— I know that since you were born, your mother said you were sick, so one problem gets fixed, and another arises. And there's this thing about having to be perfect, because otherwise I'll disappoint people. If I disappoint them, "wow, I'm so guilty," and if I'm so guilty, then...

— I'm not to blame if things don't work out for everyone, said Amanda.

— And where did you learn that? Who taught you that you have to be perfect and control everything, Amanda?

— I used to think my mother was perfect, that she had total control, that she knew how to solve everything. She solved everyone's problems.

— And you had to be the same?

— Oh, Esly... No, I don't have to be the same, do I? I have to let people figure things out in their own way, not mine.

— If you're not perfect, if you make a mistake, what could happen if you disappoint people?

— Oh, I'll be like the other seven billion people in the world. — They both laughed.

— And is that a problem?

— No, I'll be normal. Especially because other people have disappointed me too. — Amanda answered thoughtfully.

— And did you die because of that?

— No. Oh, I want to let go of this need to control, because it exhausts me.

The therapist guided her toward an image of release and empowerment:

— So then, Amanda, how are we going to do this? How will you let go?

Amanda remained silent for a long while, keeping her eyes on the activation point and breathing deeply.

— An image comes to me of handing out a little key to each person. Like: you have the key to your life, you have yours, you have yours, and I have mine. — She gestured with her hands as if distributing something.

— I like that, I think it's great! And what about those weights that were around you?

— It's like in my drawing... I had put all these little thought bubbles, each with a weight, and now it's like those thoughts are evaporating, going away, leaving my head.

— Is it better?

— Yes, my head feels lighter.

Silence lingered for a while. Amanda's expression was shifting as the session progressed. Her shoulders, once tense, now relaxed.

— Amanda, now look at that eight-year-old little girl. How is she doing?

— I can see Amanda at eight... She's eating ice cream, happy. That feeling is good. It means my problem is healed; I won't have to keep taking medicine anymore.

— And does she have to be perfect?

— No, of course not.

— Does she have to be like her mother?

— No.

— And does she have to always be sick?

— No, no.

— Because here's another thing: she's still been sick up until today—she just changed illnesses.

— Right, I don't need that anymore. The illness was already taken out back then, with that surgery, and now I can be who I am without illness. Without escaping, without migraines.

— Tell me about your throat—is there anything still open?

— No, I see the stitches closed. — She frowned, as if she couldn't fully grasp what she was seeing.

— Now that she no longer has tonsils to cause high fevers, what will happen when that little girl gets angry, when she feels she has to be perfect and is afraid she can't handle things, and the headache wants to come back?

— I have the right to be angry, I have the right to speak up, I have the right to be imperfect, without any burden. — Amanda's face was now relaxed.

— And will people still like you?

— Oh yes, I'm already loved.

— Are you sure?

— Yes, I feel loved.

— Where does all this come from? — Esly asked, and respected the long silence that followed until Amanda finally spoke.

— Maybe I didn't feel loved back then. So maybe I needed something in order to feel loved.

— Yes, but that little eight-year-old girl still seems to live inside you.

— It's okay if I don't meet expectations; my mother will still love me.

— Are you sure?

— Yes, because I wasn't always perfect, I didn't always do everything she wanted, and she still loves me.

— So we don't have to be perfect to be loved? — The therapist was "squeezing the lemon" -the core belief.

— Definitely not, because God loves me. I'm sure He knows all my flaws, even the ones that aren't visible. — Amanda's expression was completely serene.

— And will you be able to handle it when people get upset if you're angry, if you're not "good," if you don't do what they want—will you handle it?

Silence.

— Yes, I can hand them their little keys.

— Can you, or will you?

— I want to. I want to hand them over; I don't want to carry that anymore.

— Do you want to hand it over now, or only with the next headache?

— No! I want to give it to everyone! I don't want to look like I'm anyone's solution. — Amanda said firmly.

— You really aren't.

— I'm not, and I never will be... I want to let it go. I just need to be normal.

Amanda was crying, deeply moved.

— Being normal is wonderful, with flaws and virtues. Those people who act all perfect are such a bore! — Esly encouraged her with a smile.

— Long live normality!

— Long live normality!

Laughter now filled the session. The therapist then returned to the activation scale.

— Normal is so good, like the rest of the world, a human being made of flesh and blood. And now, from zero to ten, how are you feeling?

— Calm.

Amanda was breathing deeply, serene.

— And when that headache tries to come back, what will you do?

— I'll say I don't need it anymore, I want to hand over the key, I don't want to solve anyone else's problems.

— Does that feel good? From zero to ten?

— Zero, my hands aren't cold anymore.

— And is that good enough, just normal?

— Normal. — Amanda smiled.

— Follow my pointer. — The therapist started moving the pointer slowly, further away from Amanda's original activation point. — Release the spot, close your eyes for a moment, take a deep breath. (Pause.)

And how are you now?

— My shoulders are very relaxed, and so is my head. I really feel like a weight has lifted. Maybe that's why I wanted to escape — because there was no way to carry that burden. So, I would just go to sleep.

— Yes, that's how it is: we have to be who we are. And there are people who love us just the way we are — and those are the ones we want to be around. I think sometimes parents don't realize the weight they put on children when they say they have to be "good girls," they have to obey, they have to do everything just right, "don't do this, don't do that." As if there were a mold and we had to fit into it. If the head doesn't fit, the hat squeezes and it hurts.

— Yes, it's the hat that has to mold to my head.

— It has to be your hat — your size, your color, your taste. Not your mother's hat, not your father's, not your husband's, not your children's. A hat that's yours, with your name on the front.

Amanda now wore a huge smile.

— Very good, your face looks great! — Esly commented.

— It's the face of freedom.

— Now let's see how things unfold, because now you have a key — the key to your secret. You gave away the others' keys, but you still have the key to your own secret: how you need to do things your way.

— What are you taking from this session? What did you learn?

— That I can be normal. That I need to have my own way of being, without adopting anyone else's, and not resent the way I am. If I'm already loved, I don't need to run around trying to make everyone else adapt to me, or for me to adapt to them. I already have love, and I know that love truly heals.

— You are deeply loved — by your family, your husband, your children, by God.

— Yes. And I don't need escape routes anymore.

— Amanda answered with relief, wiping her face.

— We run away when we can't be who we are, when we can't express or manifest what we feel. If you can get angry, if you can be imperfect, if you can let it out when you need to, if you can say, "No, I'm not doing this that way," perhaps you won't get a headache, you won't need to escape. If your head starts to hurt, it's because the mold is too tight, because you're wearing someone else's frame. It's good to take it off, throw it away, and truly feel what you're feeling.

— Yes. And it's okay to get angry!

— Of course. Anger can generate energy for action. But if all that energy goes into running away and having headaches, you won't move forward. You need that energy to grow your practice, to grow your projects, to grow what you want to do with the church where you are serving. You need that energy — you can't do that with a headache.

— Exactly, because that's what I feel. When I have a headache, I collapse, I just want to stay quiet, I lose the whole day. I feel like when I don't have a headache, I'm a different person.

— Now you have the key to deal with what's happening inside. "Because I don't want to waste another day of my life. I don't want to be collapsed in bed for even one more day. Enough!" That's why you need this energy. This is the energy that pushes us forward. And it's going to be a learning process. You won't get it right every time, you'll probably get it wrong a lot at first. People might even look at you like, "What's going on? Who is this person?" But that's part of the learning, part of the transformation. It's what gives us the energy to make things happen.

Amanda expressed her gratitude. She felt light — and now she would carry only her own key. The weight of that one was more than enough.

Chapter 3

Ingrid's Blanket

From a very early age, Ingrid noticed that she felt colder than other people.

— I've already mentioned this to my general practitioner, to the endocrinologist... I've done several tests, even thyroid tests, since I have a little issue there, but they say it has nothing to do with it. — She furrowed her brow, rummaging through the mental records of so many appointments. — My hormones are fine, everything checks out.

The realization that her body was always the first to shrink at the slightest cold became even more evident in the courses she attended.

— I'm always wearing a sweater. I can hardly ever be without one. Then I look around and see a bunch of people without any layers at all... — She gave a half-smile, though her eyes remained serious. — Honestly, I feel colder than everyone else.

At work, the difference was noticeable too. And sometimes she wondered:

— Could this have an emotional cause I haven't discovered yet?

She had tried to explore this subject once before with another professional, without much progress. In EMDR, she had touched on it briefly, without time to go deeper. Esly asked Ingrid to adjust the lighting in the room, preparing the space for them work together online. It was time to address it.

— That's better. This technique requires us to see a bit more of the person's face and eyes.

With the new framing, the therapist invited her to explore:

— When you think about this thing of feeling cold... since when do you notice it?

— I noticed it as a teenager, but I think it goes back to childhood — Ingrid replied thoughtfully.

— Why do you think that?

— Because I have childhood memories of talking about being cold... — she said slowly. — Cold all over my body, but especially in my arms.

The therapist waited, attentive.

— Was there any specific situation?

— Yes. I do have a memory...

She searched through time with her eyes. The memory slowly reintegrated.

— I must have been in the fourth or fifth grade. It was winter. A principal walked into the classroom and looked straight at me. She said, "Little girl, aren't you cold?" That day I hasn't brought a sweater. And it was a cold day.

She hesitated.

— Actually, I don't remember if I was cold. I just remember the shame I felt.

The principal sent her to get a sweater from the office. Ingrid carried that moment with her.

— I think she thought I didn't own a sweater... And I don't know if that was true. We were struggling financially. Maybe I didn't have one, or maybe I wasn't cold. I'm not sure.

That was the earliest memory she had connected to the cold. She figured she must have been about nine years old. And she added:

— That was in a small town. I had just moved from one state to another.

When asked to rate the intensity of the memory, Ingrid answered without hesitation:

— A 7 or 8.

And where did you feel it in your body?

— In my throat.

That's where the process began. The therapist repositioned the camera, searching for the ideal spot for eye tracking in order to start with Inside Window.

— I'll look at you and call out where I see some movement. Let's see...

They began the search. With every slight movement of her eyes, a pause. A few minutes of adjustments. An occasional whispered "here." Until she found it.

— Here — she said firmly.

— From zero to ten?

— Ten.

They fine-tuned the location.

— Up higher?

— That's better,

— Lower down?

— It's bad, but the other one is worse.

Once the spot was identified, the therapist invited her to hold her gaze there and observe.

— Where do you feel it in your body?

— In my throat — she replied, her eyes welling with tears.

— Okay, keep your eyes there and just think about that for a moment.

Ingrid held her gaze fixed, and suddenly spoke:

— I can see it. I'm remembering the images...

It was recess time. Children ran across the schoolyard. Some wore sweaters, others had them tied around their waists.

— I'm without a sweater… but I'm not cold.

— But the principal said you should be cold.

Ingrid seemed to consider that statement from a new angle.

— Yes. And she was already elderly. Could it be because older people feel colder?

A silence stretched between them. Then another memory surfaced. Deeper.

— I'm remembering the move. I used to live on a farm. There I had a lot of contact with nature. There was a waterfall near my house, a river. It was close to my grandfather's place.

They moved to the big city. And with the move came disappointment.

— I was really disappointed… I thought everything was ugly. — Ingrid's voice faltered. Tears followed. — There was no river anymore… no waterfall. It was colder there than here. But I liked it there.

Curiously, she said she had been excited to come.

— But when I arrived, I didn't like anything. The house was nicer, but there was no river. Nothing anymore. No trees, no waterfall close to home. And so much car noise. The school had so many children…

She paused, absorbing the memories.

— It's strange… This memory of losing all that, I didn't know…

What was surfacing was a deep longing.

— There's a little girl living inside you who misses the countryside — Esly observed.

More images came.

— I'm remembering the second house we lived in. To this day I don't like that color, the shade of that house — it was pink. — Ingrid made a face of disgust.

It was morning, the day before school started. Her classmates came to call her at the door.

— I don't know if I didn't realize it was the first day of school... but they called me, and I jumped out of bed. I went without a sweater... and back then we wore smocks. I went out with mine all wrinkled.

The memories of clothing came back more vividly.

— Back in the countryside, we girls didn't wear pants. My mother didn't allow it.

Silence.

— The spot is a little more to the right... If you want to put the pointer down, I've already marked it on the wall — Ingrid said. — On the drawing behind you.

She looked toward the spot on the wall where she had fixed her gaze, as if anchoring a symbolic doorway there.

— Even on cold days, we weren't allowed to wear pants. — Her words came heavy with memory. — I wore dresses. Long dresses. Always below the knee. With time, we started wearing pants in the city. But when we moved from the countryside, we didn't even own pants.

— You were a different creature... — Esly joked.

— I really wanted to wear pants. — Ingrid gave a shy smile.

The therapist invited her to look again at that little girl, the girl from her memories.

— How is she now?

Ingrid replied thoughtfully:

— She's cold.

Silence settled for a moment. Then another memory came.

— The house we lived in had no lining I the ceiling. You could see the beams of the roof. You could see the roof itself. It was a very cold house.

She paused, then continued, almost in a whisper:

— One day I had a fever there. And nothing would warm me up.

The next memory came vividly.

— I remember my mother taking me to the health clinic. To get medication.

— Was this in the countryside or in the city? — the therapist asked.

— In the city. — Ingrid hesitated. — I... I don't remember ever being cold in the countryside.

She went quiet again.

— I don't know why, but I just remembered I was born in winter. I was born in June (winter in the southern hemisphere). — Ingrid kept her eyes on the spot. — And the city where I was born is really cold. According to my mother, the birth was difficult. I took a long time to be born.

The therapist asked gently but directly:

— And that baby... did she feel cold?

Ingrid took a moment.

— Maybe she did... — she answered.

— Look at her.

And after a moment of observation, she added:

— She must have felt really cold. It was June... a mountain town... — Ingrid recalled the details she had lived with in her earliest years.

The therapist suggested, softly:

— How about we go bundle her up?

Ingrid nodded. Her eyes softened.

— I see her wrapped in a swaddling cloth...

— But a swaddling cloth wasn't enough. No. She must have been cold. — Esly corrected.

— Exactly — she repeated, shaking her head. — It has to be one of those really furry blankets.

— That's better — the therapist agreed.

— Today I can afford to buy one of those. — Ingrid smiled proudly.

— So let's do it. You bought it at the store, and now you're going to bundle up the baby in it.

A silence full of images followed. Until Ingrid whispered, tenderly:

— I can see her all bundled up here. Her little face even got rosy. Now she's warm.

— What color is the blanket you bought for her?

— Green. — Ingrid answered, already immersed in the image. — I was inspired by a blanket I have... the one my mother gave me. It's the blanket I love the most.

She described it fondly:

— It's green velvet on one side, and on the other it's fur. Real furry, you know? It feels wonderful against the skin.

— Mhm — the therapist nodded, honoring the delicate atmosphere. — And did the baby like it?

— She loved it! It even made it cozier for my mother to hold that baby... — Ingrid said tenderly.

— So nice, right? — the therapist smiled.

— Yes.

She seemed to see the scene before her eyes. The image of the baby, warm and embraced.

— And this baby is growing. Growing... growing there in the countryside — Esly suggested. — She's going to play in the river. Barefoot. At the waterfall. Very free, very happy. And it's not cold.

— Without being cold — Ingrid repeated, as an inner certainty.

— And now comes the time when she's going to another city. To live. Her parents decided to move to the big city. They said it was necessary.

There was more silence.

— At the time... I was happy before we came. Afterward, not anymore. Now, knowing what I know today, that I like it here... but I see that, back then, I was really disappointed. — Ingrid looked inward. — I'm also remembering a scene at school. When I went wearing sandals that had been mended with nails.

She paused for a long time, emotional.

— I think my parents' financial situation then wasn't good at all.

Then she added:

— It got better over time. But in the beginning it was really hard.

— In the beginning, it usually is harder — the therapist said.

— The principal was right. I really didn't have a sweater.

The therapist received the recognition and offered a new perspective:

— More than anything, it seems like it was an act of love from the principal. Of care and compassion. She saw you.

Ingrid's face tightened.

— But I didn't go get the sweater. I was so embarrassed.

Silence.

— You preferred to stay cold, Ingrid. And you're still cold to this day.

The therapist listened attentively, unhurried.

— So... most likely, that day, I really did feel cold. Everyone else was wearing sweaters. I must have been cold, too. But the shame... the shame was stronger.

The therapist proposed gently:

— What if you told that little girl to go get the sweater the school office? You go with her.

— Wow... that's really hard. But it's possible... — Ingrid took a deep breath. — I called her in a discreet way. We can hide. No one needs to know.

— No one needs to know that you're going to school with the sweater you got as a donation from the school office.

The therapist then suggested:

— We can look at the heart of that principal. She saw you needed something and wanted to give it to you. You know, just this morning I saw another little girl? She wanted things, and her mother wouldn't give them. Here, you need things... and you don't want to go get them. If you like, I'll go with you.

44

— She's already talking to the principal. On her own.

— Did the principal give you the sweater?

— Three — said Ingrid, her eyes shining, fixed on the spot. — Three sweaters, she gave me three sweaters.

— Three?

— Yes. One sweatshirt, one lighter knit, and one wool, thicker.

— For all kinds of weather, right?

— I saw a bag of clothes there.

— I think some people knew a few kids were in need... generous people. And did she try on the sweaters?

— She put the lightest one on right away to go home. It was like a little blazer, you know? Very easy to wear.

— And when she got home? Asked the therapist.

— She showed her mother. Her mother was happy. Thought it was pretty. Asked her to try on the others.

— And it seems the little girl liked them too.

— Yes — Ingrid confirmed. And her mother praised her. Said she looked really cute. She kept looking at the clothes... It was like getting new clothes. And the mother said they needed to wash them first.

— Yes. It feels so good to get new clothes. (Pause.) How's the cold now?

— Better. It's warm.

— And now, when you think of all this... from zero to ten, how much does it bother you?

— Zero. Even my hands are warm. My feet too, they were always freezing. My apartment is chilly... but now it's really warm! — she said, smiling in surprise.

The therapist revisited the shift in perspective:

— It seems that little girl has understood that the principal didn't say that to humiliate her... but to care for her.

— Yes — Ingrid said with conviction.

45

— It was love, concern, care.

— Yes. She was a good person. That's why she was the principal — Ingrid added, moved. — Because she could see the children.

— Shall we go see what happens the next day? Perhaps we could go thank the principal? Both of you. The child and the adult.

— She's wearing the little sweatshirt, the warmest one. Fuzzy on the inside. I walk her halfway there. And she keeps talking. I even remember the principal's last name, people used to call her by it.

— And what does the little girl say?

— She talks to the secretary. Says she wants to speak with the principal. The secretary asks what about. And she answers: "It's about something I talked to her about yesterday. I don't want to say what it is."

The therapist listened in silence.

— The secretary goes into the office and calls her out. The principal opens the door. And the little girl goes in. Tiny. Everyone used to say she was very small. She's wearing a dress below the knee. Little open sandals. But she's warm. Everything feels warm. She comes in, long hair, and says: "I came to say thank you so much for the sweaters you gave me yesterday. I'm wearing one today. I wore the other one home yesterday. My mom already washed it. Tomorrow I'll wear another. One for each day." The principal smiled. And she asks: "Now are you warm?" And the little girl answers: "I'm very warm." And I walk away happy.

— Now close your eyes for a moment — the therapist asked.

Ingrid obeyed immediately, her face already softened by the experience.

— And see where you're going to keep this warmth inside your body.

She smiled, eyes closed.

— In my heart. And it will radiate through my whole body forever.

The silence that followed was warm, literally.

— I'll never again feel the cold like I used to — she said, her voice choked with relief. — Now I'm warm. My throat feels better.

She burst out laughing.

— That big green blanket... it's covering me now. I'm so hot!

— Feels good, doesn't it? — the therapist remarked.

— It feels great. So good! — Ingrid touched her own arms. — I'm hot. You know those little folds? They're sweating. As if that big blanket were really on top of me.

She took a deep breath and laughed, moved.

— My God... I'm going to feel all this warmth! Now I'll have to reprocess the heat! Oh my, how wonderful this is. So good!

Then she placed her hand on her chest.

— Thank you so much! From the bottom of my heart. I'm so happy and I am perfectly warm.

Part 2

Brainspotting Sessions with One-Eye Focusing on the Resource Eye

Chapter 4

Rest in Peace

This session took place during the COVID-19 pandemic, in 2020. Ruth arrived carrying a constant unease: the anxiety of moving to another city. She began talking about it right away, speaking quickly, as if she needed to unload something that had been building up for a long time.

— I've set my mind on moving south. Got it stuck in my head, as my husband says. I want to move there… I get anxious just thinking about it.

She explained that her husband resisted the idea. He said it wasn't the right time because of the pandemic.

— He said: "Not this year. Because of the quarantine, everything's complicated. We still have things to resolve here. Next year, we can talk about it." But I can't stand it. I told him: "We've been here for two years, so let's spend two years there and get to know other places, closer to other countries." But I'm obsessed. I keep looking at apartments there all the time, sending them to him. And he says: "In January we'll start talking." But then I go and send another one anyway.

She took a deep breath, showing that her distress went beyond a simple desire to move.

— Things are fine here, you know? I live in a great apartment, close to the beach… but I just can't get it out of my head. This anxiety doesn't make sense, but it's strong. Since March I've been locked up at home, life is so still. It's hugely distressful.

Esly asked what she imagined would change by moving south.

— It's just that here it's so far away. To get to a big city, to see people, you have to take a train. This place feels like the countryside. I miss living downtown. In the city it's super expensive, we'd only be able to rent a one-bedroom apartment. But in the south, with the same rent we pay here, I could get something more central... it's cheaper.

She paused and added, almost dreamily:

— I want to be able to walk, get a coffee, see people, shops. Here we don't have that. The sidewalk is narrow, you either walk in the street or on the sidewalk. And to get to the beach, you have to walk a kilometer and a half. It's ugly. I don't like it here.

It was inevitable to return to the past.

— I lived many years in my home country, near the beach. I was never able to go back to that area, and it's always been a frustration. There it was the same thing: dependence on a car. And here, I fell into the same trap. I wanted an old building, but downtown. To be in the city, with life around. But I chose a new, recently built apartment, and only later realized I was repeating the same pattern that happened in my childhood, when my parents moved to another neighborhood.

Ruth spoke sincerely, with a touch of frustration. The quarantine seemed to have intensified old dissatisfactions.

— Since March, I only go from the bedroom to the living room, from the living room to the office. Where we live surveillance is very strict. Now, with the second wave of the virus, no one can leave at all. If you do, the police come. It feels like house arrest. That's made my anxiety worse. My husband asks me the same thing you did: "What will change if we go south?" And I answer: I'll be able to walk. See people. I miss that.

The therapist commented that it sounded like something she used to do in her home country, but Ruth corrected her:

— No. Only until I was fifteen, when I lived near the beach. After that, my father bought a house in a faraway neighborhood, and my life became a gated community. My daughters grew up that way too. When I took them to the beach, they would say, "Wow, Mom, what a fun trip!" We lived in the same city but in different worlds.

She realized this, in her own words, only after moving to this new country.

— I chose this new apartment, we were charmed by it on the very first visit. But I would've preferred something old, in a downtown building. At the time, I didn't see it as a need. Now I do.

The therapist asked if this was a definitive decision — to live in another country.

— I've always worked as a psychologist. My husband was a public servant and now he's retired. My sister is here, my brother too. My whole family, my siblings, they're all here. My daughters are abroad — in other countries, studying. That was their choice. But where we are now makes the most sense today.

She explained that, for legal reasons, she couldn't work, but here she was able to do that.

— Okay then — the doctor said. — What's the bottom line? When you think in terms of house arrest… quarantine… what comes up for you?

— Social isolation. My tendency is to isolate myself. In the first months of quarantine, I even felt relief. Peace. I didn't have to go to gatherings, I didn't have to deal with social anxiety. It was fine staying in my little corner. But now… now I'm completely isolated. I saw very few people in 2020. Just me and my husband, 24 hours a day. And the dogs. I miss people. Interaction. I feel stranded.

— What was your resource spot in the body when we did the exercise?

— It was my head… it was interesting, it was almost immediate, my head was very peaceful, I was feeling stabbing pains in my chest, I noticed that during the exercise. But when I focused on the head, my chest calmed down.

The therapist instructed her to cover one eye and say the level of activation.

— Eight — she answered with her left eye covered. When she switched sides: — Four.

— Then let's work with that one — the therapist indicated, referring to the less activated side.

The client lived in a different country and had not received the Brainspotting goggles, so she used a sleeping mask to cover her eyes. She laughed as she adjusted the mask she used to sleep with in order to block the vision in one eye.

The therapist began moving the pointer in front of Ruth's eyes, guiding it slowly from one side to the other, while asking her to identify the point of greatest calm.

— Think: "I'm here under house arrest, with my husband 24 hours a day, without seeing anyone, without going anywhere." Do you feel calmer when you look here? — she asked, moving the pointer to the right. — Or more toward the center? Or more here? — she said, moving the stimulus to the left.

Ruth followed with her gaze.

— That's it... the more to this side, the better, lighter — Ruth indicated, pointing to her left.

— More to this side? Let me get comfortable. Like this?

— Let me try the middle... more toward the middle. That's it, there.

— And higher up? — the therapist raised the pointer.

— No.

— More toward the center? Or lower down?

— More toward the middle — Ruth replied firmly.

— In the middle, ok. And thinking about all of this... how intense is the activation now?

— Five.

— And if you look through the spot, out into the distance?

— One.

— One? Then we'll work with the distant point.

Ruth confirmed with a slight nod.

— Think about all of this... about this sense of house arrest, everything you described; what's difficult... and this desire to change your life. Let's see what comes up.

Silent for a few seconds, Ruth sighed.

— I feel a lack of freedom... a need to feel free to come and go. I don't have the courage to drive in the big city. I've driven since I was eighteen in my home country where traffic is crazy, fine, but here... here I didn't dare. So, I depend on my husband to take me anywhere. What comes first is that desire: to be free again. And also, to put a little distance from him. It's hard. We've never spent so much time together. He retired and we moved here in the same month. We've been glued together 24 hours a day for two years. If I go anywhere, he goes with me. It's suffocating.

— Think about that for a moment — the therapist suggested.

— Then the thought comes that the place won't fix it. That this has to be solved inside me. Anywhere will be the same if I don't change internally.

— So, take a little walk inside yourself. See where, in there, this change needs to happen, said the therapist.

Ruth dove inward in silence for a few moments, keeping her eye on the spot.

— There's something in the way I relate to people. It needs to change. I keep blaming him for being so clingy with me, but I myself don't cultivate other relationships. I have friends here, even more than in my country, but I avoid them.

— Think about that: why do you avoid them?

— Another thing comes up... I'm a workaholic. Any plan that doesn't involve something important feels empty. That's hard for me. I don't know how to deal with 'doing nothing.'

— Yeah, like having fun... said the therapist.

— Being able to have fun... — she repeated, thoughtful. — Then another issue comes in: the feeling of not being productive. And the fear of being punished for that.

— Ruth, go back in there... Your whole story lives in there. See: when and with whom did you learn that being idle, not being productive, is a bad thing?

Ruth took a deep breath.

— My father and my mother. Both of them. My father used to say I shouldn't depend on any man. He always projected on me the image of a successful person. And my mother, even though she was dependent on him, reinforced that. She told me never to be like her. It was so demanding: study, work, produce. When I met them, they only valued that. My father wanted to know what I was studying, how many patients I had. He'd knock on wood, tell me not to tell anyone. He introduced me as "the psychoanalytic daughter." It was too much. Once I arrived at my analysis and the therapist said I had inherited my father's office... it was true. The psychoanalysis office was his. He's dead now. My mother too, twenty years ago. And I'm still...

— Obeying...

— Obeying. — Ruth confirmed, her voice thick. — They're not here anymore and I'm still functioning only in my professional role. That's very hard. I always dreamed of living in a small town, with simpler parents, something I never had. When I went to the countryside and saw people eating little cakes with coffee, strolling in the square, that simplicity gave me peace. Happiness. I wish I'd had that life. Now I realize this big city has taken me to the same place as before, without simplicity. Maybe that's why I so want to go south. I'm searching for my internal simplicity. To stop. To relax. Because I don't stop. I don't allow myself to stop.

— Where is that internal engine that can never stop? Look inside and see.

— It's the need to be loved. To be admired...

The therapist looked at her with firmness and kindness.

— I think we need to talk to your father and your mother.

The mood had shifted. The agitation present at the beginning of the session seemed to give way to a calm spreading through Ruth's body; she sat more loosely in the chair, her eye still fixed on the resource spot. Despite the lightness, the emotion was intense.

— This was supposed to be a simple exercise, right? — Ruth commented with a wry smile. Resource spot... yeah, I know, but you're right.

— Are you up for it? — the therapist asked, gently.

— Uh-huh — she answered, taking a deep breath.

— Let's go in, see where they live inside you. Who do you want to speak to first?

— My mother.

The therapist guided her with compassionate authority:

— Look, this thing about disobeying parents is complicated... but if we can reframe it and see it as growth, a "becoming independent," an "individuation," right? Still, to really leave home you need two things: their blessing and their permission. How can we negotiate that with your mother? Explain to her that, on one hand, you don't want to follow the same path of being only a housewife and wife—no matter how valuable that is—and on the other hand you want to be able to rest too, without falling into the opposite extreme.

The therapist paused.

— Think about it in there for a bit. Reprocess. Talk to her however you think best — the therapist said.

A recurring memory emerged: the phone ringing early in the morning.

— Very hard — she murmured. — It was always her calling. My mother, all my life, called me early. All my married life... I left home at twenty-one... and every day she called in the morning to tell me everything she had already done. Walked in the condo, went to the market, got some sun. And how could I ever be asleep at that hour?

She sighed, keeping her eye on the spot.

— I'm a night person, I work until midnight, but I wake up feeling guilty. Even working late, I set an alarm. If I sleep past nine in the morning, the guilt comes: "You shouldn't be sleeping."

— That was her job, right? She didn't work until midnight — the therapist reminded her.

— Yeah... but I always thought they thought I was lazy... that I didn't want anything serious. That image hits me strongly. That's why it's hard to talk to her... her voice still feels imposing.

— Then think about that for a moment — the therapist guided patiently.

Silence stretched, until Ruth took a deep breath and began speaking as if she were truly facing her mother:

— I talked to her. I asked her blessing to let me rest. I explained to her that I've worked hard, that I'm successful in what I do. That I've already earned my income, recognition, which was what she wanted for me. That I can rest. I asked if she will allow me to do that. I told her I've achieved things she didn't, that I'm professionally fulfilled, that I have financial independence. I showed her the difference between us. I feel fulfilled. And now, at fifty, I can take a break. Because I've worked very hard since she passed away.

— And... Did you ask her to stop calling?

— That's it! I will ask her to stop calling.

— So you can sleep.(Silence.)

— She agreed. She's laughing.

— That's it. Your mother will hang up. And you won't answer her anymore, at least not so early. "Don't call me."

Ruth laughed at the idea, her eyes watery.

— Exactly.

The therapist guided her once more, empathetically:

— You know... sometimes we need to recognize that she also accomplished things. And be grateful.

— Yes. She did things differently... but it was her way of seeking my approval. "Look what I managed to do... I don't work outside, but I work."

— And now?

— With her, I think it's settled. — Ruth responded after a few moments.

— She will have her own rest. And you will be able to rest too.

— Yes...

— Agreed? — the therapist asked.

— Agreed. She also needs to rest. That's true.

— Does it feel right?

— Uh-huh.

— On a scale from zero to ten?

— Zero.

Ruth took a deep breath. The therapist suggested one more step:

— And now let's talk to your father. Look inside and see where he lives within you.

She paused for a few seconds before responding:

— That one... is a strong superego. My head is confused, I don't even know where to start the conversation. My eye is burning, the heavier eye... I don't know what arguments to use with him. It feels like he's saying: "I won't let you."

— Wow — the therapist murmured, surprised.

— "You're not allowed."

— Then ask him: why not? Why won't he let you? What's missing?

Ruth remained silent for a while. Then, in a deeper voice, she responded as if hearing the words echoing inside herself:

— He says: "You are just like me. You won't manage to do that. We're the same."

— Won't manage what?

— To calm down. He never calmed down until he died. Always wanting more, more, more. Always busy. He couldn't relax either.

— And all that voracity... was it good for him?

— No. It killed him. My parents died very young. I didn't have the chance to see them grow old and retire, relaxed. My mother died at fifty-two, my father at seventy. He still had a lot of vitality. He was at the height of his career, a lawyer. I didn't see my parents aging and relaxing. Always very productive, each in their own way.

— And that's the life you want for yourself?

— No. Absolutely not. Rationally, I want to drink tea and eat little cakes... but I can't.

— But he won't let you... Look, you'll be seventy and still working until midnight. — The therapist directed her to see the unpromising future.

— Yeah. And every weekend...

— Weekends, seeing people...

— Taking courses... — Ruth added.

— Courses, emergencies, I don't know what else... until it kills you.

Ruth exhaled, as if realizing the truth of it all.

— Now I see that it's not the south I want, and it's not a small town that will solve this. It's this work imperative itself. It's internal.

— What was your father's name?

— Roberto.

— "Doctor" Roberto.

— That's right. Everyone just called him "Doctor."

The therapist continued, taking on a new role:

— So? Do you want to keep being Doctor Roberto's daughter or do you want to be Ruth?

— Ruth.

— I don't quite understand... Be him a little. Be your father, Doctor Roberto. (A pause while Ruth assumed her father's role.) Doctor Roberto, you know something? Your daughter Ruth came to talk to me because she had a situation that needed a little help. She told me that you don't allow her to live her own life, to relax, to calm down, to just *be* sometimes. You know she's brilliant, right? Explain to me, Doctor Roberto, why won't you let her?

Ruth assumed her father's voice:

— Because I see myself in her. She's exactly like me. Ruth can't be satisfied. She's never satisfied. Always wants more, more, more.

— Is that yours or hers? Just because she's like you, does she have to do things the way you did? You were the one never satisfied.

— She has potential. She needs to show the world her potential. She's much more than she shows, but she doesn't know how to show it.

— And she has to show it how? By working more?

— She has to push herself more to work less.

— And if she does that, will you let go of her?

— Yes. If I see that she's earning well, not depending on her husband for anything, I'll allow it.

— And why can't she depend on her husband? Explain that reasoning.

— Because men are not reliable. And he's at an age where, if he finds a young girl, he'll leave her. And she'll have nothing.

— And did you do that to your wife?

— I cheated on my wife my whole life. But I never abandoned my family. Never. But I wanted to many times. I know men. None are trustworthy. All men cheat. So, I don't want my daughter dependent on any man.

The therapist nodded, understanding the distorted logic of protection.

— So, what I see is that even as a man, you don't know how to retire. She told me you worked until seventy, until you dropped dead.

— That was right, wasn't it?

— Men don't really retire, do they? Asked the therapist.

— If they retire, they die. I preferred to die working than be an invalid. My fear was depending on others, get stuck in a bed, depending on my children. That was my fear. — Ruth still kept the deep, fatherly voice.

— So, in a way, you lived as you wanted. And died as you wanted.

— Uh-huh.

— Great. Now I'll tell you something: not everyone can do that. Congratulations.

— Yes. I died with dignity. That's what I wanted. I didn't lose my dignity.

— And productivity, right? All your life.

— Yes.

— So... does Ruth need to do the same?

— Yes. We have to have dignity. We can't depend on anyone in this life.

Esly observed Ruth attentively, guiding the conversation with the inner father:

— Is there some way? I was explaining to her... When we leave home, we need both blessing and permission...so we can do what we want in life. Truly wishing the best for the children... We've already instructed, guided, given advice. I know she married young and all that. Is there a way for you to give her the blessing, the permission for her to be Ruth and do things her way?

Ruth responded slowly, as if hearing her father's voice from inside:

— I need to distance myself from her, so I don't influence her. For her to be herself, I need to step back.

— But you live in there... Try to negotiate with her. I'm talking to Doctor Roberto inside you, you're already there. Because sometimes, people leave home without permission. They give the blessing, but not the permission. Other times, they go, but without blessing. And she wants your approval, your permission to do things her way. She's very tired. I don't know if you realize it, since you haven't seen her in twenty years... But she's already achieved a lot. Financial independence, a good husband, raised her daughters... studying abroad... even your granddaughter is studying medicine!

— Yeah... Ruth was supposed to be a doctor, as I wanted. I couldn't become a doctor because I got caught cheating on the entrance exam. But my whole family is full of doctors. Ruth was supposed to be the family doctor. But she did this damn psychology thing that just adorns my office. I put a psychology certificate just for decoration. All my life I said to her: "Do medicine, do medicine."

— She had to do what you failed to do?

— Yes. She was very smart. She even skipped grades. Taught herself to read. She was the genius of the family. She had to be the doctor to make me proud.

— But I'll tell you something: that's really unfair. Imposing on her what you failed to do. She's the one who has to go on carrying all that?

— I always saw myself in her. That I know.

— But she's tired of living your life. She came here to talk to me and said: "I'm tired of living this life." I'm talking to you to see if you'll let her. But if you don't, it's fine. She'll find another way.

Ruth fell silent for a moment. Then her voice softened:

— Yeah... I'm thinking here. Even though I'm a frustrated non-doctor, I was a very happy lawyer. Always said: "Good thing I didn't pass the medicine exams, because I managed to be happy." And I see that she's a very happy psychologist. Today I recognize that. She made the right choice for herself.

— Hmm... is that a blessing? — the therapist asked.

— Yes, that's a blessing. Because she managed to be very good at what she does. And she even achieved financial independence. I never believed psychology would give her that. And she did it.

— The same thing happened to me. They said I'd starve as a psychologist. And here I am.

— Yes. I always thought it wasn't a profession for her to succeed in.

— Look, you haven't seen her in twenty years. But I see your daughter. She's doing very well. Shall we let her be a psychologist? Don't you want her to be happy?

— Yes, of course. I want her to be very happy.

— Isn't it better to have a happy psychologist daughter than an unhappy doctor?

— Uh-huh. And I have a granddaughter now who will be a doctor.

— Now you have your granddaughter to do what you wanted. Done. Shall we send her a little present... or not?

— No. Better not. Poor girl. Leave her. She's not doing it for me. She's doing it for herself.

— Yeah, because she wants to. So, it's fine. Shall we let Ruth do it her way? Can we, Doctor Roberto?

— Yes. Yes, we can. I can allow her to do that.

— Thank you very much, Doctor Roberto. Until next time.

The therapist asked Ruth to close her eyes as she returned to her own role. She asked her to listen to what her inner father had said. Ruth obeyed, moved.

— He understands now. He understands that I found my path. He said he only wanted me to find my way in life. And he saw that I found it. So, now he's calm. He apologized. He said he wanted my best, he didn't know he was harming me. I feel relief now.

— And the eye? Go back to the point. How is it now?

— I'm relaxed.

— From zero to ten, how is it?

— There's a little... I don't know... one, maybe.

— So think about it a little. Feel it. Look at the point.

— This one is really mine. Ruth already knows this. She's been released. I just have to let go. — Ruth was silent for a minute, then added: — It went down. Now it's zero. Calm.

The therapist smiled and asked gently:

— So, Ruth, what shall we do now? Stay where you are? ...Or move to the south?

— For now, I'll just relax here. Try to have a calmer life here. I'll wait for my husband to get to that point in his own time.

— And if he doesn't come?

— If he doesn't come, it's because I'm meant to stay here. This place is wonderful too. I just need to find other ways to achieve what I want. It's not as extreme as I made it at the beginning. There's a lot around here too.

— Sometimes we also have to give ourselves the blessing and permission to enjoy what we have.

— Yes.

During the final conversation, Ruth began reflecting on how she could make better use of her time in this place.

— Think about that a little, if it's possible to do that with Ruth. — Esly suggested.

— Yes, I'm thinking about this period I'm here, what I can do to enjoy it better.

— And do you have to leave?

— No, I don't have to leave.

— Do you have to have all that voracity?

— No, here there are very good things, I have many friends here, I have a beautiful beach in front of me, which they don't have in the south, here there's a really blue sky.

— So let's enjoy this here first, because now you won't have early morning phone calls, the phone won't ring anymore, and now you have permission to reorganize your schedule the way you want, since your father freed you. He thinks now you have professional judgment to decide for yourself, I even heard him say that.

— It's already making me want to explore other places nearby — Ruth was excited.

— Great!

— The nearest city center is half an hour away. I can go there, have an ice cream...

— That's it. Not this afternoon, but maybe tomorrow.

— Yes, tomorrow is Monday, I already thought, Monday doesn't work. But it can, another day right? — Ruth now smiled.

— Yes, it can! Why not? Are you good like this?

— Yes.

— Release the spot, close your eyes, store all this inside you wherever you want, wherever you can access it whenever you need.

— So much peace I'm feeling.

— That's great!

— Thank you.

The therapist drew Ruth's attention to a curious detail on a shelf behind her:

— Just a little thing, I don't know if you can see it on the video behind you, look at the black figure in the middle.

— The little black monkey?

— From where I see it, it doesn't look like a monkey. It looks like a person resting. I kept looking and thought: look, isn't that rest right there, and she didn't see it?

— That's true, that's true. From where you're seeing it, it looks like that, right? — Ruth tilted her torso and head, as if half lying down.

— Yes, from here it does. How are you feeling now?

— Ah, I'm great! — Ruth's shoulders were relaxed.

— Yes, it was necessary to release both mother and father so they could rest too. Isn't it like "rest in peace"? So, rest!

— True, they both need it.

— Yes, they don't need to keep watching you, following you around all the time, or calling every morning.

— I loved that, I asked her to stop calling me, it was great!

The therapist shared something personal, creating an emotional connection resonating with Ruth's experience:

— Yes, I thought it was better to ask, you know, because I think many of us, successful women, in this generation — and I'm from a slightly earlier generation, which also thinks it's exceptional — we had parents like that, you know? Who really valued intelligence. "Oh, Esly is intelligent," you know? And it's hard to stop and rest.

— Yes, because my sister, she was beautiful. She was the pretty one at school and I was the smart one, so I got that role, I had to be the smart one, the one who would actually become a doctor, and that was very strong in my life.

— So, congratulations! Good rests and good schedule rearrangements.

— Later I'll send some photos and post in the group of me out and about. — Ruth seemed like a completely different person; her expression had totally changed.

— I know you won't stay idle, but you'll learn to have periods of rest, right? The Bible teaches that we must have Sabbath. One day in seven we must rest, otherwise we can't produce. So, choose one day and rest, okay?

— Okay. Agreed.

Chapter 5
Delivering the Pizza

Lilian came into the session very determined. There was an issue that had followed her throughout her professional trajectory and seemed resistant to time, even after twenty-three years of a successful career. As soon as she arrived, she began to speak,:

— I want to work on a professional issue... I graduated twenty-three years ago, and ever since then, I've always worked in the field. I started in HR and then alternated between HR and clinical work. What I notice is that today I have a block, when giving a lecture or presentation, teaching a course. I have to prepare a lot, I mean really a lot, for that situation. And even then, after preparing, when the time comes, it feels mechanical. It doesn't flow naturally.

She made short pauses, as if trying to reorganize thoughts that, at the right moment, stubbornly refused to appear.

— Sometimes I want to say things, explain, and I can't. Then, when I step off stage, it's like all the insights come rushing in. "Wow, I should have said that...!" When it's time to give the show, I don't give the show. And after it's over, a lot of things come to mind.

This freezing of ideas wasn't limited to stages or training sessions. It also infiltrated her clinical work.

— This happens in therapy too. When I'm with a patient, sometimes I get stuck. And when the session ends, I think: "Wow, they wanted to say this… this connects with that other thing." But at that moment, at the right time, the thoughts freeze.

— You feel like you have a lot of history — the therapist observed.

— I do, and when it's time to show it off, to show that I know, that I understand, that I get it. And I keep giving trainings. But it freezes. It's like I can't be the star on stage when I'm on stage.

She sighed, as if speaking about an internal character she knew well, but on whom she couldn't rely in decisive moments.

— I want to show this ability at the right time, because sometimes we miss the timing.

— And the moment has already passed, right?

— Exactly. Even if I come back with insights afterward, it's too late. Sometimes I feel like I miss the timing of things, and with that, I'm not recognized. People don't see who I really am. And I feel bad about that. Because my thoughts froze, and I couldn't give the show.

— And everyone loses the benefit of the good things you have to offer…

— Exactly! My insights, my creativity, my thinking. I think outside the box. I'm creative. But when it's time to show that… it seems to freeze. And only comes back when I step off stage.

Esly brought a different perspective, anchoring Lilian's words in concepts from psychodrama and other approaches, which speak about "tense field" and "relaxed field" states.

— One very interesting thing we talk about in psychodrama, which comes from other areas too, is that our creativity really flourishes, grows, and appears in a relaxed field. The tense field, on the other hand, freezes us up. We don't function well. This happens to everyone.

She shared her own experience of public speaking, something familiar to Lilian, to illustrate the idea.

— In the first two, three, four minutes, nervousness makes us stay in the tense field. You stand up, see a huge audience — three thousand people, who knows — and those first few minutes are tense. That's fine. The problem is staying stuck in that state. We have to find a way to enter the relaxed field, because that's when things appear.

Lilian listened attentively while Esly continued, encouraging practical reflection.

— What I feel is that you enter the tense field and don't get out of it. Think about that, see how you can develop ways to relax.

She paused and illustrated with the popularity of live streams.

— In the past, on TV, everything had to be perfect, a thousand rehearsals. Today, with YouTube or Facebook live streams, people don't mind if the dog barks, or if you make a mistake. They want to see the real person. That's important for you to think about.

Esly asked Lilian to close her eyes, directing her attention to her body.

— I want you to find a relaxed spot within yourself, a resource, a place where, when you are well, these insights appear. For this to happen, you need to be relaxed. Where is that in your body?

Lilian reflected for a moment.

— I think in my legs, my feet. From the waist up, everything is tense: heart racing, stomach, mind running. So, I guess from the waist down.

— Can you be more specific?

— The legs.

— The soles of your feet, knees, right leg, or left? Let's pick a well-defined spot.

— Right leg.

— Great. Are you wearing your glasses?

— Yes.

— I want you to think about this difficulty you described. Now cover one eye and then the other. Cover the right eye.

Lilian complied.

— Thinking about this difficulty, on a scale from zero to ten, how much activation do you feel?

— Six — Lilian replied.

— Now the other eye?

— Eight.

— Okay. So, let's focus on your resource eye, the left eye.

Lilian lightly wiped her eyes. Esly continued:

— First, let's find the brainspot of highest activation. Then we look for a resource spot, a point of calm. When you think about this topic, where do you feel the most activation? (Esly raised the pointer and started moving it across the client's field of vision, seeking out the brainspots.) More to the right, center, or left?

— I think in the middle, center.

— And is it higher, middle, or lower?

— More in the middle.

— Here?

— Yes.

— Okay, let's stay at this place. Now let's find a spot where you feel calmer, less activation. Is it more to the right, center, or left?

— More toward the corner.

— Here?

— Yes.

— Higher, middle, or lower?

— Higher.

— Here?

— Yes.

— This will be our resource point.

Esly indicated the point with the pointer.

— Now look at this point. Thinking about this difficulty, how much do you feel you're in that place?

— About four.

— Now look through that point, toward the wall, and tell me how much disturbance you feel over there.

— Two.

— I'll hold the pointer here to maintain this spot. You know you have a resource in your right leg, and if needed, we'll work with your resource eye at this point and distance.

She invited Lilian to reflect more on the block that prevented her from "giving the show," from expressing herself as she wanted.

— What comes up?

— I get the feeling that I'm not good enough.

Esly asked her to go deeper:

— Where do you think you learned that? When, with whom, at what age?

Lilian remembered:

— I think it's a memory from fourth grade, when I got my first failing grade. I came home crying from school, afraid to tell my mother. Then I told her.

Esly asked how much that memory bothered Lilian at the moment, on a scale from zero to ten.

— Six — she replied.

— Tell me, why did it bother you so much?

Lilian reflected:

— Fear of disappointing my mother. And also disappointing myself. I think these points, when not activated, end up blocking me.

— Could it be?

— I can't see much, you know?

Esly reminded her that, when we are in a tense field, we can't act well.

— Where do you think you learned that?

Lilian pondered.

— I think because others can do it, and I can't.

— Hmm... What do you mean by that?

— I'm not sure. I learned that with effort, we can achieve anything. I put in the effort to get everything I want. Even so, sometimes it doesn't work out.

Esly commented:

— It seems like your effort isn't enough, like something is missing. What could be missing?

— I don't know... the word that comes to mind is fear... maybe courage? But I see that I do have courage.

Esly brought up what Lilian had said about disappointing her mother and not meeting expectations.

— When we focus more on how we'll present ourselves to others than on our content, when we worry too much about the "failing grade," it gets in the way, right?

— Uh-huh. I worry about others' judgment.

— And then, where does your focus go?

— I shouldn't get blocked, right? Why does it block me? I prepared. I think it's not just the expectation of others, it's mine too...

— So, where is your focus? — Esly pressed a bit more.

— On the other person. I shouldn't be afraid of the other, of others, but why this fear? Fear of criticism, being judged, punished.

— Could be. Fear of failing a test.

— Ah, yes... — Lilian gave an awkward smile — Failing, being rejected...

— Rejected. You end up being rejected in situations where you could have been accepted easily.

— Exactly. Even being fired, because I was fired for this, not for lack of competence, but because I didn't give the show.

Lilian acknowledged that, ultimately, what mattered was the show, not the ability itself, but how the show was delivered.

— What matters is the show you give out there.

Esly added, speaking about delivery:

— You know, you can have everything prepared, everything ready, but you have to deliver. You have to "deliver." When you get there, you need to give it to the people. Could be a show, maybe not a show, but there has to be delivery. You delivered, like when someone buys a pizza: the person has to receive the pizza.

Lilian made a comparison, trying to internalize the idea:

— Yes, but you know when you deliver and say, "this is my delivery," but there are people you look at and think: "ah, that one knows how to sell." Like, I'm going to sell a pen, and I say: "this pen is blue." Other people say: "this blue pen does this, does that," but their delivery isn't as good as mine. The advertisement is good, but the delivery isn't.

Esly offered a different image:

— The image that comes to me is this: I bought a pizza, you delivered half of it. Where's the other half? I asked for the whole pizza.

Lilian responded:

— But it's you who aren't seeing the whole pizza; the pizza is there.

— But I was promised a whole pizza — Esly insisted. — I called, ordered the pizza that way, baked this way, with so many slices. Then you come and give me half a pizza. I say, "What do you mean half a pizza? You can't make a whole pizza? Since when do you sell half a pizza?" You say: "Ah, I'll bring the rest later." "Later I don't want it anymore; it'll be ruined."

Lilian tried to explain:

— But I tried to make the whole pizza.

— But you only delivered half — Esly observed.

— And what do I do to deliver the whole pizza?

— What do you think can be done? How do we do this? — Esly asked.

— I want to deliver the whole pizza. I want you to be satisfied — Lilian affirmed.

— Do you want to deliver the whole pizza, or do you want me to be satisfied? — Esly pressed.

— Both. I want to deliver the whole pizza and for you to be satisfied — Lilian assured.

— Exactly. When you leave the pizzeria, do you have the whole pizza or not? — Esly asked.

— A whole pizza — she replied.

— So, what happened along the way? You got on the motorbike to deliver the pizza. What happened to the other half?

Lilian gave a simple answer:

— Focus.

— Focus on what? Focus on whom? — Esly asked for details.

— Focus on the delivery, focus on the order.

Esly shared a personal example:

— Yesterday, when I went downstairs for lunch, my husband said: "I ordered an apple pie you like." We had lunch, and when we opened the pie, obviously it had taken a tumble. The pieces were all there, but upside down. He turned it and said: "Looks like an apple crumble," which is made in little pieces. We didn't send it back because everything was there; what mattered to me was eating the pie. But it had taken a tumble, for sure. If I were pickier, I would have sent it back: "Hey, the guy delivered the pie upside down!" But the pie was tasty; I ate it anyway. Now, if it were a pizza, I don't know if I'd accept it upside down. What do you understand from this?

— I understand it's about the delivery. There's no point in making the pizza if you don't deliver it the way it's supposed to be.

— Sometimes you can even deliver it upside down, and if it tastes good, we'll eat it. But sometimes the pizza has to be exactly what the customer expects. Did all the slices arrive? Half a pizza? No, sorry. If I were to talk to that delivery guy, what advice would I give him, so he doesn't mess it up again? Because I'm a kind customer. What advice would I give? — Esly encouraged Lilian to reflect.

— That he should be more careful, know what he's carrying, pay more attention, have more focus on what he's doing.

— Is it difficult to deliver a pizza? What's harder: making a pizza or delivering a pizza?

— Making it takes time.

— Making takes time, effort, preparation — Esly agreed. — You have to make the dough, put the cheese, the ingredients the people want, bake it, takes time, then put it in the box to deliver. Is it hard to reach the door, ring the bell, and deliver it?

— No.

— So why is it hard for you?

There was a moment of silence. Lilian kept her eyes on the focus.

— What blocks this delivery? Why can't I deliver the pizza? Actually, I can't deliver the pizza.

— You deliver half a pizza.

— Yes, I deliver half a pizza — Lilian confirmed.

— Because if you delivered nothing, you could even cancel the order. But you deliver half... Where did you learn that half a pizza is okay?

— I think what comes is: I prepared so much, but the delivery will go any which way, just to get it over with. I prepared so much, but I want to get rid of the delivery, I deliver it any way. I don't seem to care about it.

— It seems like it's "people will see the effort and grade you for the effort. They'll grade because you made the pizza." But that's not the rule.

— Maybe I focus on preparing, but I don't focus on delivering.

— You know that delivery is so important that in the U.S., there are clubs called Toastmasters. It's a club where you give speeches on different topics and receive constructive feedback. They evaluate you not just on content, but on delivery. Every time you say "um," they deduct a point. You'd pay five cents for every "um" you said. Delivery is that important. Your mother might give you a grade for effort, but life does not.

Lilian nodded in agreement, absorbing and reflecting.

— I get this feeling that I withdraw when it's time to deliver, I withdraw, I can't push through, right? I withdraw — she spoke with a mix of indignation and sadness.

Esly acknowledged with empathy, talking about how our behavior shifts when we get nervous.

— There are several things at play here. One is that when we get nervous, everyone regresses, right? When we enter a tense field, our less developed roles disappear. The strong roles we know well are the ones that will show up. If I'm tense, my role as a mother appears, my role as a therapist appears, but my role as an architect, which is still developing, vanishes. It's normal. Anyone entering a tense field shows their strong roles, and the underdeveloped ones disappear.

The second thing: we infantilize. The tendency is to revert to childlike behavior. That's why you need your adult role well developed; otherwise, the child role takes over: "Oh, don't do this to me, look at my effort, look, Mommy, see how well I did, I didn't deserve this grade, I studied so much for this test, didn't deserve this failing grade." "It's okay, child" — but life doesn't do that; your mother does, but life doesn't.

The third: delivery is something you learn. Did someone teach you how to deliver a pizza? No, right? Nobody taught you. I have a friend in the U.S. who got a job to pay for gas, delivering pizzas. On her first day, of course, the pizza fell. She delivered it, the customer complained, called the store. She returned to the pizza shop, and the owner asked: "Dropped your first pizza yet? Great, because everyone drops the first pizza. From now on, you can do it right; this is how you deliver a pizza." He taught her. We learn by watching and listening to others. So, how does that translate for you?

— More relaxed, more adult, to handle it, or to prepare — Lilian was searching for answers within herself.

— Prepare for what?

— Delivery.

— Delivery — the therapist reinforced.

— Because I prepare like an adult, but deliver like a child.

— That's the key. There it is. Do people want to hire someone to deliver like a child?

— No way.

— Look at my pointer and follow along — Esly moved the pointer back. — Release the spot. You can take off your glasses. How do you feel?

— Good, like an adult, I'm here.

— Understood?

— Yes. — Lilian smiled. — Yes.

Esly then shared a story. She had a friend, her wedding godmother many years ago, someone who believed in her long before she believed in herself. This friend encouraged her to do things she didn't want to do, like present in public. She refused: "I don't have the content, I don't want to." But twenty years later, the friend asked her to give a presentation. She agreed and gave a show.

— And then she asked me: "Where did you learn to do that?" I thought…

I remembered a lecturer I worked with, as an interpreter, for several years. He was super dramatic, had stage presence, funny, full of gestures, had an amazing sense of timing — knew when to speak, when to pause, when to poke. I, as an interpreter and psychodramatist, imitated him to avoid standing frozen on stage.

When my friend asked me, I realized it was him. Three, four years traveling with him, doing that work. He passed away two months ago, very young, younger than me. He received many compliments, but for me, he taught me how to… deliver pizza. Last night, I even heard him on YouTube, I don't know why he appeared there. In a few minutes, he said incredible things. I thought, he shouldn't have died yet; he had so much more to offer.

That's what I mean: we learn this. Go to Toastmasters, take public speaking classes. I know people, all shy, who went. The teacher gives three minutes of explanation, hands over the mic, says, "Present yourself," and everyone's terrified! But four or five days later, they're presenting up front. I never realized I had learned so much, but if you see me today, you'll see how much I learned from him. I'm not like him, but today I have stage presence, I know timing, I know how to tell a joke, I know how to be serious, I know how to deliver the punchline. Could be four minutes, four hours — it's not just talent, but not just effort either.

Lilian listened attentively.

— Nobody will grade you for effort, only your mother will. She says: "Don't worry, next time you'll do well." Life doesn't. If I deliver pizza like the apple pie yesterday, I give a course only once. Nobody pays for the second time. Got it? Now the challenge is to learn how to do it, because this is learned.

Let me give you some tips: watch YouTube, TV, pay attention to TED Talks, find people you admire, think: "When I grow up, I want to be like that." Pay attention, take notes, watch and listen several times until it sinks in. I never realized this until my friend asked me where I learned to present like that. Then I saw how much I learned from him. It happened unconsciously.

Today, I might stumble a few minutes at the start, but it's the first seconds that count. I find my role in that tense field and think: "I have something to give you, a wonderful pizza I made and sold, and I baked it like this." And people respond: "Exactly, that's great, what a tasty pizza! Worth the investment." So, it's not just a show. The show is the final product, but it's all learned. It takes work, effort. If you don't deliver, you lose everything. That's why I say: I don't know how much it is a block and how much is lack of learning; it's just a role that needs to mature, grow up, learn. You'll stumble here and there, but we read the evaluations, which are so precious. I read them all.

Do you think I stopped learning when I got older? No. We need to see how to deliver the product. When we went online with basic training, I thought: "How am I going to deliver this? I've never delivered pizza like this." Then the team brainstormed, talked it through, and it worked. The first one wasn't perfect, but look, what we learned: the second one is easy; we know how to teach. Got it? Go out there and kill it!!

Part 3

Brainspotting Sessions With One-Eye Focusing On The Activation Eye

Chapter 6

Marcela's Photo Album

Marcela settled into the armchair. The memory came vivid, intense, fully present in her body.

— Well... seven years ago, I was in Asia — she said, her voice wavering slightly. — I've been there a few times, doing humanitarian work with vulnerable children. On this second trip, I went to one of those countries.

She paused, as if reliving very specific images. The return to Brazil, however, had not been as expected.

— When I came back, I was very sick. Really unwell.

Since then, the symptoms came in waves. Marcela's speech unfolded like a carefully assembled puzzle, piece by piece.

— When I got back, I started experiencing some severe physiological symptoms... right after returning from Asia. I went to several doctors — infectious disease specialists, neurologists — because at first, I had hypoglycemia.

She emphasized that she had never had hypoglycemia before.

— I had to go to the hospital to get glucose intravenously because I lost strength. I lost physical control completely.

The hypoglycemia lasted two months. But it was only the beginning. New symptoms followed, one after another.

— I would have one issue for two months, then it would change. I had problems controlling my sphincters... couldn't control my bowels. Doctors suspected multiple sclerosis. Later, I experienced total paralysis.

Marcela spoke clearly, as if she had recounted these events many times before, but the impact of retelling was still evident.

— I recovered, but after three or four months, it all came back. I underwent tons of tests in several places. They never found exactly what it was, but the MRI showed cerebral demyelination.

The initial suspicion of multiple sclerosis was discarded by different specialists. A more stable diagnosis came later: cerebral vasculitis.

— Today, I treat it as cerebral vasculitis. I've recovered all functions... but I also had speech problems, swapping words, aphasia. And that unfolded over months... even years.

She estimated that during the first three years after the trip, all the symptoms had manifested. In the fourth year, she began treatment that brought significant improvement.

— When I started treating the demyelination... I improved a lot.

At this point, Esly intervened.

— So, you finally got an accurate diagnosis?

Marcela nodded. But the story didn't end there.

— Four months ago, I got COVID. And with COVID, the left-side hemiparesis returned. I still have difficulty today.

She had no doubts about the origin of it all.

— I believe the origin is traumatic. All the doctors say: "You went through a traumatic situation." I think so too.

— Do you think so, or do you know? — Esly asked gently.

— I know so! — Marcela replied firmly. — I went through several traumatic situations in Asia.

There was silence between the sentences, heavy with meaning. She knew this would only be the beginning of a long session.

— In summary, that's it — she said, as if she knew the summary didn't do justice to the story.

Esly nodded empathetically.

84

— Look, it would take a four- or five-hour session to really get everything done. But let's see what we can do with the time we have. Maybe we can offer a little relief to your body too.

Esly paused, looking carefully at Marcela, as if inviting her without forcing.

— So... you said you went through several situations in Asia that affected you. Shall we start at the origin?

Marcela nodded silently.

— Since your inner doctor thinks it started there... and your Inner Psychologist agrees — Esly said with a kind smile.

Marcela let out a brief, almost relieved laugh.

— Then we'll start with your Inner Doctor — the therapist continued. — Is there a specific situation you want to start with? The first, the worst, or all of them?

— They're all tangled together — Marcela replied with a tired sigh. — All at once.

— You don't need to describe what happened, okay? — Esly explained. — But give me one or two words so I know where we're heading.

Marcela took a deep breath. The word came quickly, sharply:

— Helplessness.

Esly simply repeated it, holding the space the word opened:

— Helplessness.

The room quieted. Something inside Marcela began to move. She adjusted her glasses as she prepared to dive into the memory. The memory of Asia still pulsed, alive in her body, even after so many years.

— I was in Asia... and I went alone — she began. — Initially, I went alone.

Being a woman already placed her in a vulnerable position. Going alone to that specific place made everything even more delicate. Marcela recalled the arduous process she had faced to be there. She had encountered difficulties as a brown-skinned woman in Brazil, but she was light enough to be seen as white in Asia, which carried a dangerous expectation.

— There, they thought I was rich.

She traveled to another city, further north, a difficult-to-reach region. She worked in neighboring towns, with vulnerable women, and later with orphaned children.

— At some point, I had to cross by boat to get there, you know? It was quite risky.

Reaching the orphanages required even more — motorcycles, makeshift trucks, precarious routes. The images came back in an avalanche.

— A lot... so much information — Esly acknowledged gently. — But enough.

She guided her back to the present, to her body.

— When you think of all this, how disturbing is it now? When you think of the Asia chapter of your life?

Marcela searched within herself for an answer.

— A five, now.

— "Now"? Why? Is it higher or lower?

— What bothers me most is my lack of mobility today — Marcela replied, slightly shifting focus.

Esly gently pressed:

— When you think of the Asia chapter... is it a five now because it used to be higher or because it used to be lower?

— Much higher. — Marcela sighed. — It reached an eight, nine...

— And when you think of that eight or nine... where do you feel it in your body?

— Tightness in my chest.

They tested with the left eye, covering it with her hand, getting a SUDS of 3. With the right eye, a SUDS of 7. Esly gave Marcela the choice of which eye to start with; she preferred the right eye, the one more activated.

— Do you have your glasses with you? — Esly asked.

After a few adjustments with the camera, reflection, and computer positioning, the exercise began.

— Think about your seven. And look here — Esly guided the pointer along the horizontal axis — does the tip bother you more here? Or here?

They tested point by point, making millimetric adjustments to the discomfort. With each movement of the pointer, Marcela reacted.

— More here? Higher? — Esly adjusted along the vertical axis.

Until she nodded:

— There… more or less.

— Is this good?

— Perfect.

Esly prepared for the dive.

— So, I want you to think about this seven. Think about this Asia chapter. Feel it in your body. And let's see what appears.

Silence extended. Until Marcela's voice broke out, in a nervous laugh:

— My heart is racing.

— Tell your heart it's okay — Esly replied. — You're not in danger. We're just remembering.

Marcela remained silent for a few moments, until the memory began to form with perfect clarity.

— I remember going there — she said, eyes fixed on the point. — Since I was alone, I went through some difficult situations at the airports.

This experience in Asia was etched in her memory. A whole day, twenty-four hours, waiting for a connection that seemed never to arrive. Alone, exhausted, unwell.

— Many people came to me asking for things — she continued. — And I couldn't use the bathroom because I couldn't leave my luggage. And my throat hurt, I wasn't feeling well...

Her voice oscillated between narration and the memory reactivating in her body.

— I couldn't use the bathroom... the risk of theft was too high.

The next memory was even more unsettling.

— I brought many books because we were doing a training with teachers. I'm a pedagogue... — She paused. — But the police thought I was carrying drugs.

She was detained, searched, experiencing fear that went beyond embarrassment.

— They held me at the airport until they checked all my luggage. Then they saw it really was books, but in the meantime, I missed my flight... and there was no other flight to where I needed to go. And I didn't know anyone there.

She tried to ask for help. No one allowed her to use the phone. Her own cell phone, set up for international calls, failed.

— I was very scared. Couldn't give anyone any news — she concluded. — And all of that... all of it comes back to my chest.

Esly followed with full presence. She waited silently.

— Now it's a little calmer... my heart rate has slowed — said Marcela after a while.

But new images appeared, like windows opening one after another.

— Scenes come to me... of some children.

She recalled the home visits. Mud floors, no sanitation. Five children, motionless, silent.

— They couldn't speak. They were malnourished — she said, her voice breaking. — The neighbor said they were waiting for their grandfather. He had gone a week ago to get food. He hadn't returned.

Marcela breathed deeply. The pain was intense in the memory, visible on her face.

— I wanted to take them with me. Adopt them. Feed them. But I couldn't.

The scene hurt more than words.

— It was a feeling of helplessness. The children were so small... so thin. And so hungry they couldn't even talk to me.

The silence was heavy now, loaded with sadness that would not dissolve.

— I also remembered when we went to attend women with AIDS.

There were several who brought stories of abuse, violence, abandonment.

— The men in that region had about five women. And many of these women told stories... stories of pain. Many couldn't feed their children or take care of their health. They suffered a lot.

Esly, in a low voice, returned the question that naturally arose:

— And what does all this do to you?

Marcela took her time but responded firmly:

— It brings a feeling of helplessness. Like I feel when... when I can't walk.

She searched for the right word.

— Paralysis... — suggested Esly.

— Paralysis!

The silence lasted several minutes.

— I just remembered a situation... — said Marcela, her eye still fixed on the point in front of her. — I went to give a lecture... There were women from eighteen communities gathered there.

It was an important meeting. A regional group had organized so the team could get there. But the journey, as usual, wasn't simple.

— Either you went by motorcycle... or one of those trucks, you know? Like a bus, but everyone squished on top. — She inhaled deeply. — We opted for the motorcycle.

She was traveling with a small group, though some people had gone ahead. She went on a motorcycle driven by a driver. Behind her, another light-skinned man from Marcela's team, with a local pilot.

— I'm brown, right? But there I was the lightest, and my colleague on the other motorcycle too... and the two... the two drivers diverted the path.

She paused. The memory now manifested not just in words, but in tense expressions.

— It was as if they were trying to kidnap us. I screamed... they spoke another language. I didn't understand anything.

Marcela and the other man screamed, called for help. No one listened. Until someone from their group realized they had left the route. They were rescued.

— It was also a feeling of helplessness — she said softly. — Fear... a deep fear. Of not being able to do anything.

— Was it really a kidnapping attempt? — asked Esly carefully.

— It was.

Silence settled again. The therapist waited respectfully. Then she resumed:

— How is it now from 0 to 10?

— A four... — Marcela replied. — Thinking... no.

— No?

— Thinking about it, it went up. Physiologically, my heart is calmer, but the situation itself... I'd say a seven.

She shook her head, trying to push the images away. But others were coming.

— And now, when you think about all of that, how much does it bother you? — Esly asked softly, maintaining presence and tenderness.

— It got worse thinking about not knowing what was happening... what they were going to do with me... — Marcela said, her voice trembling. — It's already going up to nine now.

— What else scares you about it?

— Not being able to ask for help. No one could hear me. And I didn't know where they were taking me. It was a desert. Lots of destruction everywhere.

After a few seconds, a new memory emerged without Esly needing to ask.

— I remembered another difficult situation too...

It was another crossing, this time by boat. Nothing was safe.

— It was very precarious. Very cramped. So many people. There was a man telling us to squeeze together to get through faster. And the river... it felt like I was going to die there.

Even accompanied by familiar people, the fear was visceral.

— It was so scary. So scary.

Esly observed, waiting with tenderness and presence.

— And now? — she asked quietly. — From 0 to 10?

Marcela took a deep breath, checking in with her body.

— Eight.

— I just remembered... — Marcela began, in a calmer tone. — That despite everything, the mission I had there... I accomplished everything I was supposed to do. I gave the lectures. Everything that needed to be done, I did it. I did it with great care.

But soon after, her firmness dissolved.

— But on the way back... I couldn't wait to get to Brazil. I was very sick... already on the way. And I really wanted to see my family. So much.

She sighed, as if reliving the exact feeling of that return.

— When I arrived at the airport... no one was there to meet me. That was very sad for me. Because I had such a strong desire to see my family. I went through so many difficult situations... so much vulnerability...

— Did they know you were arriving? — Esly asked.

— Yes, they knew.

— And why didn't they come?

— The airport was in another city. My parents are elderly, so... they couldn't come. My sister was sick. They could have arranged someone, but...

She wiped her eyes.

— I really missed them. I saw other families welcoming arrivals. And I... I was so homesick...

The therapist just nodded, present.

— I felt helpless, you know? There... and here. Arriving at the airport and having no one there, from the people I love most...

— From 0 to 10? — Esly asked.

— Seven.

The session continued in silence for a few moments. Then the therapist leaned slightly forward and said:

— I want to make you a proposal, Marcela. And you can say no.

Marcela nodded, curious.

— I want to propose that you redo this whole trip. The one you just told me about. How long did it last again?

— Two months — Marcela replied. — That was the most traumatic one.

— Was it the first one?

— No, it was the last one. Definitely.

— Definitely the last one, right? — Esly said with a smile.

Marcela nodded.

— This is what I want to propose — Esly said, in a symbolic tone. — I want you to redo this memory now. But with two conditions. The first: our whole team that is were with us, goes with you. You're not going alone. I'll go with you. Other psychologists will go. Doctors, men, women... a whole team. Wherever you go, we all go with you. And everyone will help you.

Marcela took a deep breath. Something in her expression began to ease.

— And when you go through this path again — Esly said gently — I want you to tell that Marcela who went to Asia, who lives inside there… that she no longer lives there. That she is no longer in danger. She never has to go back there.

Marcela blinked several times, touched. Her eyes poured out her feelings in a torrent.

— That it was terrible, yes. But it's over! She survived. She was brave.

— Yes — murmured Marcela, almost like a child who needed to hear it.

— Despite all the risks, she did everything she had to do as well. But the price was high.

— Yes.

— Can we do that? — Esly asked.

— Yes.

— Everyone is here. Ready. Everyone is boarding with Marcela. So, let's go. I'm coming along. Let's go down to the airport with you. And you'll go through the whole path…

Marcela thought for a moment. She felt safe again.

— I feel very safe!

She paused for a long moment, breathing more easily.

— It's something different… — she said, almost in astonishment. — But in our team, there are men.

She gave a small smile, as if beginning to perceive a new scenario forming inside herself.

— That is very important there. Because there… women are very… Here in Brazil, we are privileged. We have a voice. There, women speak, and no one listens.

She gestured with her hands, as if trying to explain the inexplicable.

— They shout, telling you to shut up.

She remembered with vivid clarity.

— When I arrived there, the drug issue... they only told me to shut up. I wanted to say it wasn't drugs. I wanted to call someone. But they wouldn't allow it. — Her voice trembled, tears streaming down her face, now slightly contorted by crying.

— But here, there are men. Here there are men who can represent you. There are even doctors. There are men. The phone works! — Esly said excitedly. — You are not alone.

— I also have professional partners. Professional partners — she repeated, with conviction.

— I am surrounded by capable people supporting me.

She was still crying, but a bit of relief came with this perspective.

Silence again, until she continued:

— There, I was able to get in touch. After a long time, I got the contact of someone who eventually took me to her house and cared for me. But if I had that whole team... I think it would have been very different.

— Yes — Esly confirmed.

— The place I went to was also very difficult. But with the team, it would have been different. Maybe I wouldn't even need to go where I went. We could even stay at the airport.

— At the airport, we would have organized ourselves and everyone would go to the hotel.

— Yes. — Marcela smiled with mild irony, without bitterness. — If they allowed it, because there they weren't allowing it. But with the team, they would.

— And what is it like with a whole team at an airport? — Esly teased lightly. — We'll have a party! We'll sing... They'll watch your bags for you when you go to the bathroom.

— Yes! — Marcela smiled.

There was a glimmer of humor in her voice now, but soon her expression grew serious again:

— They won't let me be vulnerable, because some men came... it was... unbelievable... They were making propositions.

She shook her head, disapprovingly.

— One man came, then another… and I felt awful… it was a very delicate situation. Because it wasn't a flirtation. It was coarse, very disrespectful and invasive.

— But they can't even get close to you now— Esly said.

— No, there are so many people. We're more than 20 here.

— Yes.

Marcela was silent for a moment. Her eyes overflowed:

— And it hurts to see those children… and not be able to do anything for them.

Esly intervened:

— But you know what? Our team is so careful. Colleagues have made little sandwiches, milk… Everyone has food for them. And they'll put it in the cupboard so they can eat until their grandfather arrives.

— I brought some things. But… the children couldn't swallow. Because they didn't have the strength to swallow. — Marcela's eyes still streamed tears.

— But here there's a doctor — Esly reinforced firmly — and they know what they're doing. They're guiding us. And these children will eat.

— Very good to imagine that. To think that those children won't starve…

But soon came the sobering thought:

— Probably the grandfather wouldn't return.

Marcela took a deep breath, trying to dry her face.

— But with the team, we could get those children to some safe place. Let's go! — Esly said. — Let's take them to an orphanage!

Marcela nodded gently.

— Those places I went to… I believe that if I had the whole team, we wouldn't have gone the way we did.

— Imagine going by motorcycle… exposing ourselves to those men… We wouldn't have been in danger at all.

— Yes. — Marcela laughed, remembering her own impulsive courage. — And still laughing. Like I did many times. In some humanitarian work here in Brazil. It was very different.

She recalled another experience.

— The first time... the other time I went to Asia too... they were safer places. People came to me, not the other way around.

There was a silence, and Marcela sighed, as if a new field of memory was opening.

— I also have very good memories from there. Not everything was bad.

She smiled, tenderly.

— I went to an orphanage where they had seventy children. And there... they were given food.

She paused.

— And now there are seventy-five, right? — Esly said.

— Yes. — Marcela continued, moved. — They had food, a clinic... There was also a school. They learned. I was able to teach them many things. I do ventriloquism work. And so... they laughed a lot. They had fun. — She paused, emotional. — I think it was very impactful. It was very good.

Her tone was lighter now, warmed by the positive memories.

— I also remembered the lecture with the women. I think it was eighteen communities... I don't remember exactly. But there were many women.

She made a wide gesture, as if she could still see those women gathered in front of her.

— And I did a good job, a lecture... and it was very beautiful.

Her expression transformed as she recounted:

— At the time, a person in charge told me that maybe the women wouldn't give much importance to what I was going to say. Because they didn't give much importance to someone without children. And I don't have children. But even though I'm not a mother, they respected me. They honored me. They listened. It was very beautiful. The learning… the richness created there, in knowledge and pedagogy.

— You managed to leave a legacy — said Esly.

— I couldn't continue working with the children, but I trained the teachers there. From the orphanage and other places, other schools too. I gave a very good training.

— So, what you planted there… stayed?

— Yes.

— And it kept multiplying?

— Yes. That was my purpose. I wanted to multiply my pedagogical knowledge. To give them something… for them to multiply. So, I trained people to continue the work. It was very beautiful.

— It's still beautiful, isn't it? — Esly commented.

— I see the photos of what they've been doing there. And it's very rewarding to see the seeds that were planted. It was very beautiful.

— Was all that effort worth it?

— It was worth it.

— A much better picture, right?

— Definitely.

— A brief silence. Then Marcela added, her voice firm:

— And a lot of gratitude. They had so much gratitude.

She remembered a special gesture:

— When I left, they made kind of a map of the region. And many women signed it. Families… because I worked a lot with families.

Her eyes welled up.

— It was such a beautiful tribute they made, full of gratitude for the work. From both teachers and families.

She took a deep breath before concluding:

— I may not have helped those five specific children… but in some way, I contributed.

— Definitely.

Esly then proposed:

— And now… when you think about the Asia chapter, how does it feel from zero to ten?

— Much lighter. Two.

Esly smiled warmly.

— Then I'll make you another proposal. When we take a trip, and when we come back… we make a photo album of our journey.

— Yes.

— We choose what to keep. This past weekend I went to my sister-in-law's wedding. She's 80. Widowed. And she married a man… also 80. They don't even look that old. I took a ton of pictures. Now I'm putting together the photo album I want to make for her. I think: "this one stays, this one goes, this one is beautiful, this one didn't turn out." And the nice thing is now we can choose the photos we want, only what we like.

Esly looked at her more firmly:

— I want you to make a photo album now of your experience in Asia. What do you really want to keep?

Marcela nodded confidently.

— Let's remove the photos we don't need. We don't need to keep remembering the almost kidnapping. We don't need to remember all that.

A silence fell.

— I can bring to mind the things that give me hope.

— Then start taking out the photos you don't want — Esly guided lightly — and keep the ones you do.

Marcela was silent again. She seemed to be flipping through an invisible album, removing pale, blurry, or ugly photos.

— There are so many beautiful photos — she said gently.

— I'm sure!

She began naming the images appearing in her memory.

— The children's laughter. Smiling with me…

— Our photos nowadays have sound, smell, temperature. They're not like old photos. Now we open them and they move.

— The orphanage children hugging me... You can always feel the hug.

— Joy — Esly added.

— Contentment.

Marcela continued:

— Some families giving me food... Sometimes I would think I wanted to eat an orange. They didn't have it, but somehow they found one... I just thought it. I didn't even tell them. Suddenly, they came with food. People, so much love — she said, still surprised by the memory. — So much care. They didn't have it for themselves. But they were bringing it to me.

She paused, emotional.

— It's more blessed to give than to receive... Wow. And some houses I went to were very poor. But there was so much love. This photo has feeling too. So much love. I received so much love. From the children. From the families. Many couples...

Her face, still flooded, now showed an open smile.

— The whole team came to mind... Everyone taking pictures with me. Everyone with me.

— Happy that we completed the mission — Esly followed her rhythm.

— We completed the mission. The team went. The team stayed with me the whole time.

— And now we are going home — Esly added. — Marcela, we're taking a bus. From the airport. And we're all going together. We'll take you to your parents' house. Deliver you there.

— Alright.

— You won't make this journey alone. And it will be that wonderful chaos! Your parents will be amazed too. Wondering who this whole team is... "Ah, it's the team that accompanied me."

There was another pause as she imagined it.

— I arrived well. I liked it. I'm safe. They welcomed me warmly. Especially since I was well accompanied.

— Yes, I think they even made coffee, I'm sure!

— Definitely. Some cheese... They welcomed everyone.

Esly looked at her warmly and asked:

— Now, when you look at your photo album... of Asia... how does it look?

— Much nicer.

— And how much does this chapter bother you, from zero to ten?

Marcela smiled without hesitation:

— Zero.

Esly, holding the pointer, moved the pointer back:

— Follow the movement... Now release the spot.

Marcela took a deep breath, closing her eyes.

— Switch glasses — Esly said as she obeyed the gesture.

Marcela put on the glasses covering her right eye.

— Missing a little towel, huh? — she said, smiling, her face soaked, trying to dab with her hands.

— Oh, I can't help with that. I can't reach for the Kleenex from here online. — Esly laughed. — And now... when you think about the Asia chapter, how does it feel?

Marcela's whole body seemed lighter.

— Much better — she said after a long silence. — My heart is calm.

— From zero to ten?

— Zero now.

She nodded, as if seeing the photo album she had been building throughout the session.

— This album... you have it with you now? — the therapist asked.

— Yes. It's very present.

— Then let's find its brainspot here for you to keep?

Marcela searched for the glasses in her bag and commented with a slight laugh:

— Can I put on my prescription glasses? It's hard to visualize.

— Sure! I don't have that issue... That's why I like these big glasses, we put them on top.

— It's hard to see the point with this eye. — She adjusted the Brainspotting glasses over her prescription glasses. — Now it's better.

They adjusted the new point, Esly indicating with the pointer and Marcela following along.

— I'll go a little to the left... To the right... Here?

— Yes, closer to the letters. — She pointed to a spot in the back.

— Look below and check if it's not there... Also a bit higher.

— Here?

— Yes.

The therapist watched her attentively.

— When you think of this album now, full of all these beautiful photos... What word comes to mind?

Marcela smiled.

— Gratitude.

— You had such beautiful words... Gratitude — Esly repeated. — So, what I want you to do is imagine that this gratitude, from this spot where you are now, radiates to every part of your body that was affected.

Some time passed.

— I'm feeling something in my legs — she murmured. — I can't explain what it is...

— That's okay, you don't need to explain.

— But it's something good.

After a few minutes of silence, Marcela added:

— My left arm too.

And then, in a low voice, as if surprised by her own body:

— It's as if my heart feels warmer.

— And it is warmed!

— And it flows through the blood, right? Goes through the whole body.

— Exactly. — Esly said firmly — Now you don't need paralysis anymore.

— No.

— Because now you've already arrived home with the team. And you're safe. You're no longer trapped.

Marcela added:

— Yes! And my metabolic system will work normally too.

— It will. You are no longer powerless. You no longer have paralysis, nor lack of anything.

— Only gratitude.

— No helplessness. No fear. Now it's gratitude. And gratitude heals.

The therapist then suggested:

— Now I want you to take a pause here... In your brain. In those areas the doctors said had demyelination... I want you to wrap those neural fibers with gratitude. Because they don't need to stay exposed anymore. And you don't need to keep suffering. You're home.

— Yes. I worked hard to develop neuroplasticity... But now I don't need so much effort, right?

— Now it's easy. Just wrap it in gratitude.

— I'm home. I'm safe. I'm no longer in danger. That's over. I kept the good things.

She took a deep breath.

— It's very good. This feeling is very good.

— It really is.

Marcela concluded, with a new serenity in her voice:

— And the feeling that I did what I could.

— You did. You contributed. And it was worth it.

— It was. Absolutely.

— A drop in the ocean. But this drop helped a lot of people. And it continues helping today.

— Yes... That's how I feel. I did the best I could.

— You gave them your best.

— Yes.

— So ,you don't need to keep punishing or lamenting yourself. You did well.

— I am grateful to God for that. — Marcela added, eyes welling: — Grateful to you too.

The therapist then proposed a collective image:

— And this gratitude, we are all putting it into a big, inexhaustible pot of gratitude. We are grateful that you shared this experience with us.

— I'm thankful for you traveling through this experience with me.

— And we can still be part of this story now... — The therapist smiled tenderly. — Whenever you feel a little prick, you open our little pot of gratitude, the one we're giving you, and place it there, wrap the neurons... Talk to your body and say: "Hey, none of that is true anymore. We live in Brazil. We're home. We're okay. We're no longer exposed. We're safe."

She confirmed:

— Do you see it? Are you noticing it?

— Yes.

— Then close your eyes for a moment and keep it.

Marcela inhaled deeply, eyes closed, as if sealing a treasure in her body.

— See where you want to keep this inside your body: your photo album... And the medicinal pot of gratitude. Inexhaustible. Whenever you need it.

A long, silent pause followed. The therapist suggested:

— Try it. Put a little more in your arm, in your leg, in your brain... An extra dose today.

— I sent it to myself, right into my heart. Already distributed throughout the body... pumping through the blood... and everything is well nourished.

Marcela finished with a relieved smile:

— It will work well now. Everything will work well. Because that's over. And it ended well.

— You can take off the glasses... This album had a happy ending.

— Yes. Thank you. It has a happy ending. Yes.

— So, what are you taking home today?

Marcela answered, her voice still slightly choked:

— Lots of gratitude. Lots of love. Lots of peace. Support.

— Support! There are so many people here with you.

— Yes. Absolutely.

— You know, when we go through an experience like this, critical, like we did with you? It unites us. It creates intimacy. Because now we are comrades in arms. In crisis. We faced all of this together. We accompanied you. We went together to Asia. And we brought you back, everyone together.

— That's wonderful... Thank you! — Tears still ran down Marcela's face.

— Now you are safe. And whenever you need, call, really call.

— Thank you.

The therapist suggested:

— Shall we go back to our class?

— Let's. Just let me compose myself...

She slowly moved away. The therapist spoke in a playful tone:

— But don't go far! Stay listening!

Marcela laughed, still emotional:

— No, I'm just going to grab a little handkerchief over here.

While Marcela stepped out for a moment, the therapist turned to the group:

— While she grabs the handkerchief, I want you to keep this in mind... First, we're going to share on a personal level. She shared with us personally. Does anyone here doubt that we went to Asia? I went!

The colleagues, now visible in the image, nodded.

— So, I want you to share with her. Where did this touch you? How does this relate to your own story? I myself want to tell you a few things, Marcela... Let's see if I can do it without crying... My mother had demyelination, and it took over 40 years to discover what it was and to recover.

She paused, breathing between words that came out in an unstable tone:

— Look where you ended up... — Esly smiled, eyes glistening. — And one of my deepest wishes... from my heart... was precisely to be able to bring healing to some of the more suffering places, like Asia or Africa. And it's the same places you went. The same thing you wanted to do. And the pandemic allowed us to do it. We've already brought healing. We were able to bring EMDR... And now they are coming here to take the Brainspotting course as well. So ,I wanted to tell you how much I admire you. For going, for doing this. And the good seed you planted... it's planted there, bearing fruit.

Then, other colleagues also shared words of support and recognition, expanding the circle of empathy built throughout the session.

The meeting ended in a climate of deep acceptance. Marcela thanked them, moved, saying she felt, with intensity and truth, the support offered by each one.

Chapter 7

The Shimmering Magic Potion

Marta arrived talking about the pain that had accompanied her for just over a year—a lumbar disc herniation that hadn't eased despite medication, physiotherapy, orthopedics, Pilates, and acupuncture.

— It improves a little, but I can't get an effective result — she explained, referring to the long hours she had spent sitting, during the past months of the COVID-19 pandemic. She added, with conviction, that the pain no longer seemed to be just a postural issue.

The therapist suggested starting by clearly locating the pain area. She asked Marta to cover one eye at a time and rate the activation of the pain on a scale from zero to ten for each eye.

— With the right eye covered... Nine. It even makes me feel a bit nauseous.

— And with the other?

— Five.

They agreed to work first with the more activated eye. Marta adjusted the glasses so that the left eye, the one with the higher score, remained open. The therapist lifted the pointer and positioned herself against a neutral background to avoid distractions.

— Without moving your head, just follow with your eyes. Where does the activation feel strongest: more to the right... center... or left?

The pointer slowly moved across the visual field—right, center, left—until Marta spoke up:

— Can I say something? This point here — she said, pointing to the right — my heart speeds up, my breathing becomes stronger. That's what I really notice changing... and the urge to blink increases.

— Uhum. So shall we stay with this one? — asked the therapist, moving the pointer to the right.

— A little more this way.

— And now? More up, more in the middle, or more down?

— Lower. The breathing gets stronger there. — Marta's expression was already changing.

— Okay. Think about this pain, where it is in your body. Look at this point, and let's see what comes up.

Marta fixed her eyes in the indicated direction. Soon the images began to appear.

— It's... what came up immediately was the memory of the trip I took last May for a course. The scene, you know? Before I got to the hotel, even before the course started, I stopped at a pharmacy at the airport and bought a bunch of medicine, everything I thought might help. I didn't want to feel pain. I was going to be at the course for three days and I was very afraid I wouldn't manage — she took a deep breath, her voice slightly trembling. — And I didn't even yet know that it was a disc herniation.

— Okay.

— The scene came so clearly... me walking into the pharmacy with that strong fear of not being able to handle it. I was far from home... and I really wanted to do the course. Even my heart speeds up just thinking about it...

— Uhum. Do you have any idea when this started? — asked the therapist. — What happened that created this disc herniation situation?

— I had already been feeling some joint pains for a while — Marta replied, thoughtful. — A few months ago, I tore my rotator cuff, I think due to posture. I tore both of them, in both arms. I ended up slightly compromising the weight of my gait... I remember that. I started compensating, shifting weight from one side to the other. I had already been treating these joint pains for some time. Then I realized I hadn't taken care of myself because of that.

— Uhum... but do you have an idea what caused this hernia? What would your Inner Doctor say?

Marta paused, her eyes still fixed on the point.

— When you say "Inner doctor," the image of the external doctor immediately comes to mind... The external doctor said I must have had this hernia for a long time, like many people do, but not everyone feels pain. Then, when you say, "Inner Doctor," I get a sensation... of difficulty positioning myself. .. of standing up to things. Understand?

Her breathing intensified slightly.

— At the same time, when I relax too much — she continued — I sit wrong, walk wrong, don't exercise... also, with regard to people at work, I end up not positioning myself. And that causes me a lot of pain. The Inner Doctor says that. That the pain is related to not knowing how to position myself. Not knowing how to say no. Not knowing how to set boundaries. This shows up very strongly in my work sphere.

Marta furrowed her brow, as if the memory was taking shape before her.

— I remember clearly... as soon as I returned from there, I really wanted to start seeing clients by Monday. And then I fell into the trap of taking on too much, often voluntarily, without charging, seeing everyone. That EMDR workshop taught me a little about positioning myself as a professional. It taught me that the work has value, it has results... That I can, yes, do volunteer work, but not everything. Not in any context. This difficulty in positioning myself comes up very strongly. My heart even speeds up just talking about it.

The therapist nodded slightly, guiding the reflection gently:

— Some people have a lot of difficulty dealing with a "no." But it's the "no" that protects us. "No, my daughter, you're not going to cross the street without holding Mommy's hand because the car could hit you." Or "no, I won't do this because I can't handle doing everything."

She paused briefly before continuing:

— Where did you learn, or fail to learn, to deal with "no" this way? Without saying it. Without setting limits. Without positioning yourself? How old were you?

— It came... not exactly an image, but a thought — began Marta, still fixated on the point. — I'm the eldest daughter in a family with five siblings. I remember my parents owned a store, and they worked a lot... and I took care of my siblings. From a very young age.

Her voice remained steady, but the pace slowed, as if drawn by the memories.

— I remember scenes when I was eight or nine, having to take care of the house, the kitchen. So much responsibility. That got in the way a lot. Then a more specific memory came up. I was about thirteen or fourteen when an aunt had a brain aneurysm and died suddenly. She was six months pregnant; the baby also died. She left two young children, one nine months old and the other two years old. My family took the children in. We became seven.

She paused for a long moment before continuing, her breathing heavier, tears streaming down her face, one drop after the other.

— My mother kept working, my father too... and I found myself taking care of those children. I remember exactly thinking: "my adolescence is over." That's what I thought. That now I would have to change diapers, make bottles. And on top of that, the pain of losing that aunt. My hands are sweaty now, look... cold. At school, my classmates called me "old maid," can you believe it? Because I think I was extremely responsible for things I didn't need to be. I didn't need to have all that responsibility, right?

— Not really... — Esly asked gently.

— I don't think it was my responsibility — Marta replied, eyes brimming with tears. — I took care of my siblings, always worrying if they had eaten, if they went to school, if they did their homework. But I don't remember anyone taking care of me. If they did, I didn't register it. Because I did it for everyone else. And that reflects a lot in my professional life... I end up wanting to handle everything. When people seek my help, it seems like the time or the moment doesn't matter. I've changed some things, but I still have difficulty positioning myself, especially regarding values. It's as if I couldn't charge what's fair for a session.

— Uhum.

— The image of my cousin came up, the eldest boy, two years old. He cried a lot for his mother. And he always came toward me. He called me "mommy." That confused me... I didn't know what to do, and I don't remember any adult supporting him. Neither my parents nor his father — who, by the way, came to live with us. I only remember myself in all of this....

— How old were you?

— Fourteen. And now I feel heaviness in my eyes... a strong desire to close them. Pain here, look — she pointed to the side of her face. — A heavy pain

— If you need to close them a little, do it. It's a lot of pain indeed. Being a mother at fourteen, taking on all that care, without an adult nearby... it's heavy.

— My hand is sweaty...

— Uhum. And could you say no?

— No. There was no way. But a feeling comes up... a word: "pride." Today I know they are well-established. They're already men, already fathers. It makes me very proud of them, of who they have become, how they've managed life even without their mother. And with our family there, right? When I think of them today, the feeling is...

— Participation — the therapist completed. — Of having fulfilled what needed to be done. Right?

— Yes. But I also wonder: where were the adults?

— Where were they? Where were your mother and father? Asked the therapist.

— I think it was a very difficult phase for my family. In one year, we lost two uncles in a car accident, my grandmother fell ill, and then this aunt died... very traumatic losses. My parents worked a lot. My mother would leave at eight in the morning and only come home at eight at night. She lived at the store. My father too. I took on this responsibility... to handle everything.

— You had to, right?

— I had to. But today I don't want that responsibility anymore, the one that's not in my control. Today I see it clearly. I can't. I couldn't say no back then. I didn't even have the time to not want to. But today...

— Sometimes we don't even have the option, right? — said the therapist. — If we are a person of good character — as you are — we help. We do our part. The part of a mother, father, aunt, sister... Now, how about talking to that girl? You know she exists. She only exists inside you, but she's there. And she's still working hard, taking care of everything. She's fourteen. She needs to be a teenager. To grow up.

— Uhum — Marta replied softly.

— What would you say to her, now grown up, at your age? — the therapist suggested. — Like, "enough is enough." Now you can give this back to your mom and dad at the store, and grow, because that's the right thing to do. Shall we do that?

— I just need to recharge... give me a minute — Marta replied, eyes still turned inward. — Done.

— You can speak or do this silently, whichever works best for you. But she needs to hear from you: "Look, you did well. You tried your best. I am very proud of you. You sacrificed for your family, for your mom, for your dad. You helped a lot. But now you can give the letter back."

— I think what I most want to say to that girl... to that teenager... — Marta began, voice trembling — is that she gave me the feeling of being a very hardworking person. And I am hardworking. I learned that from her.

— I understand — the therapist said softly.

— I brought that into my life. A lot of work, a lot of effort. But this effort... it doesn't need to hurt. Do you understand? It doesn't need to hurt this much. Because today it hurts. The hours I spend sitting, the hours I spend doing what I didn't need to do... it hurts. But she taught me a lot. That it's possible to help. Only now... I have to help myself. I have to take care of myself. My body, my pain, my posture.

— And that she doesn't have to take care of the little siblings anymore. Because the little siblings grew up. Mommy and daddy survived. Everyone grew up. Everyone has their life. And she can receive that information. She needs to hear that from you. She will only believe it if it comes from you. She will only find peace if she hears it from you.

Marta took a deep breath, eyes moist but shining. Silence lingered for a few moments.

— Oh... such a good feeling came. Peace. Peace I hadn't felt in a long time. A relief... you know that feeling of carrying a weight that isn't yours? That image came. And it's funny... I don't know why, but I need to say it. I remembered when I helped in my parents' store, packing groceries. Sometimes we carried heavy bags to the customers' car. And that feeling came. Those bags aren't mine! I don't need to carry them.

— You did it for a while because you had to. You helped a lot. Carried bags that weren't yours. But you don't need to anymore. Done.

— Yes...

— You can let go.

— Yes... I felt that in my body, you know? Letting go from my arms. Like when you carry a plastic bag too long... — she ran her fingers along her hands and wrists, making the gesture — and the arm becomes sore. The bag even leaves a mark. And when you release it... it hurts, but it relieves. I don't have to carry it anymore!

— Yes, not anymore.

— It's physical, right? — Marta said, surprised.

113

— It's also physical — confirmed the therapist, warmly.

— Something so interesting came... — Marta said with a small smile. — I chose to be a Sunday school teacher, work in the children's ministry... and then a scene came. I think it was at school. Children playing, running in the yard. You know that feeling of watching kids running everywhere? A joy, a lightness. And while watching... it was as if I saw myself too. Playing. Among them. Running. Playing. I don't know exactly what scene it was, but I know it was recess, school. A good scene. A lightness...

— Uhum — murmured the therapist. — I have another suggestion for you, if you want.

— Okay.

— You can say no.

— Hum...

— But I think you need to talk to that aunt who passed away. Tell her how you committed, yes, to taking care of her children. That everyone assumed responsibility, but who really cared for them was you. That you were their mother. And now you want to give back to her the care for her children. Tell her how well they turned out. I'm sure she wants to know. Tell her: "I did my best. I gave my best. And I was a girl. But I gave my best. They turned out well. And I am very proud of who they became. I wanted you to know that too."

Marta closed her eyes for a moment, and the silence between them was full of presence.

— This aunt of mine... — she began, voice choked — she was very dear. Her name was Priscila. She was a Portuguese teacher. Since she joined the family, I admired her greatly. She was extremely competent, loving, caring. When she first got sick, had her first headache, I was at her house. Helping, on vacation there, because I adored her.

She took a deep breath, gaze fixed on the point ahead.

— Certainly, what I did for these children was thinking about how she would do it with her own kids. She wanted to have six children, but couldn't. She only had three. Pedrinho, who ended up dying at six months gestation. It's very clear, very clear, that the love I gave, the care, the concern... was inspired by her. It was for her. But I missed her a lot. A lot. Really a lot.

— Because it was also your pain — Esly empathized.

— Yes.

— It wasn't just for the children.

— No. With her books... everything she read, what she taught... A scene came to me. A library was founded with her name in the city where she was born. I visited that library years later, took the children there. We went to see it together. Her story was there, her memory. And that scene came. The scene of the library. The memory.

She paused for a long time. Then smiled tenderly, with longing.

— It was good to talk to her.

— Great! — said the therapist, sharing the emotion.

Once again, that feeling of satisfaction and duty fulfilled took over Marta. It was a good feeling, different from what she carried at the start of the session — a weight, a discomfort. Even her hands were calmer now.

— Yes, because amidst so much pain, sometimes your pain from losing her also gets lost — the therapist said.

— Exactly.

— And now you can let go and keep what's good.

— Yes... You know when you get a massage? That feeling of your body relaxing? I literally feel like that. It's like I had a massage. My body... it feels completely relieved...

— And now, when you think about that lower back pain, the herniated disc we started working on... From zero to ten, how is it now?

— I don't feel the pain like I did at the beginning... It was like this — she opened and closed her hand to illustrate the throbbing — Now, a two.

— Uhum. What does that two represent?

— Two... it's almost time for me to take the pain medication I've been taking every twelve hours. So I'm not sure if this two is that, you know? I'm not feeling anything now, but it's the fear of feeling it. When the course started today, I had the same worry I had in the other course. I thought: "How am I going to sit all afternoon?" So, since yesterday, knowing this, I took the medication. The two is that lingering fear. Of feeling that sharp pain, sciatic nerve shooting down the leg, tingling... But now, right now, I don't feel anything. What a relief — she exhaled deeply. — And I'm in the same position as at the beginning.

— We have a scanner inside us, a kind of CT scan. Take a look at that disc. How is it?

— This morning I went for acupuncture and told the physiotherapist I felt like I had injured this area. I said even touching it felt like it was hurt. And she said: "It is, there's a hernia, but which injury are you talking about?" I found it so interesting that she said that.

— Uhum.

— And now I understand. It was hurt.

— It was hurt, yes. Very hurt. A huge injury. So much pain.

— When I do this scan in my body and reach that area, a thought comes: "No need to stiffen, no need to tense, no need." Because I have this tendency to stiffen. But now comes this: no need.

— No need anymore. No need to carry bags, carry the child, give bottles, change diapers... No need to be the mother of those nephews and siblings.

Marta inhaled and exhaled slowly.

— The feeling I have is... I think I could sleep now.

— Nice, right?

— Very! Because an image comes. I've been to so many doctors, done so many treatments, spent so much money. Everything they recommended, I did: "Go there, do this, try that." And I always said: "It doesn't get better, it doesn't get better." But now I understand why it didn't get better.

— It was a different kind of injury. Now I'll tell you a secret. You have some magical potions. This injury you have — that only you see, only you feel, and only you have the remedy — I want you to see it. And then, in the magical cupboards you have, I want you to take the remedy this injury needs.

— I managed to visualize it. A potion appeared in my hand. An image that comes to your mind — we don't know from where, right? But it comes. A potion like this, in my hand. Because I put so many things in that place... compress, plaster, massage... But then I put this potion. And it came with a feeling, like... how much love I need to put into myself. I gave so much to others... but now I need to give this love to myself. It's the same love I gave outwardly — and I really gave it, yes? Donated it all. But now I need to put it on myself. It's mine. I need to take care. Take a potion of love for myself. You know? But I visualized this potion, like, in that place. How funny... how these scenes come...

— So much love you gave, that's why these boys turned out well, right?

— Yes. Yes.

— This wound is only yours, okay? Only you can care for it. I'm not saying this in a depreciative way. I'm very serious, and you understand: only love heals.

— Yes. — Marta replied, face still wet with tears.

— Tell that girl who was so alone, in the middle of so many children, so many responsibilities, so little adult support... She's fourteen, right? Now you've freed her from those responsibilities. She already fulfilled her role. She did very well. She deserves a medal of honor. Now we are going to take care of her. Let her grow. Let her play. Let her date. Go to school. Play in the yard... Now she doesn't have to be a young adult, nor an "old maid auntie." Enough, right?

— Enough.

— Done. From zero to ten?

— Now, with the love potion, I can see zero. I know it's possible to heal. It will get better.

117

— You're on the path, right?

— Yes. Now I can understand the two. Now I can understand the zero, too.

— Shall we switch glasses?

— Just a moment — she said, rubbing her hands over her eyes, drying them. — It was blurry... done.

— Shall we see with the other eye? Is there still pain there?

— Let me see if I can put on my glasses — she said, adjusting her prescription glasses over the Brainspotting ones. — Better now. Because that side is where I have more issues.

— Close your eyes for a moment. Go to your injury. From zero to ten, how is it?

It wasn't bothering her. Thinking about the injury no longer caused any pain. She moved her body, testing its limits.

— Can I move? I had so much pain. During the break, I stretched, did the exercises I know need to be done to keep the pain away. It wasn't yet time for the medication... May I stand up?

— You are in your home — replied the therapist, laughing.

— I don't feel the pain. It's relaxed. That massotherapy feeling, you know? I've tried so many things... osteopathy, everything ending with "therapy" or "pathy." But now, I feel no discomfort.

— Is it zero?

— It's zero. Really, this side — she pointed to her right eye — was more activated at the beginning. But now... This morning, I was really worried. I was already thinking about how to position my computer, my phone, how I would sit, turn this way or that... But it's not hurting. I don't know what will happen from now on. But right now, no, no pain.

— And now you have the magic potion.

— Literally. Oh, how beautiful. It's so interesting how the image of the hand comes... I think it's from some cartoon I saw, the hand like this — she brought the sides of her hands together, as if holding something delicate — with a magic potion full of little sparkling things, going straight to this side of my lower back, the sciatic nerve. I know there's the hernia. But I used to say: "Eighty percent of people have hernias, protrusions, wear-and-tear. It's normal, it's the spine." But why did it have to hurt so much? A doctor once told me: "And look, your hernia is very small, you know, for it to hurt this much..." He even joked: "I have patients with much more serious issues..." And I thought: "How can it hurt this much?" But now — she inhaled deeply — now it's different.

— Take off your glasses. Let's give it one more check.

— Okay, sure. Because before, when I thought about it, my heart raced, my hands sweated... Now it's all fine. "Squeezed the lemon" and it's zero.

— Great!

— Thank God! — Marta cheered.

— Very good. I'll go back to my corner. Thank you so much for being willing to share with us.

— Thank you.

— This experience... I have to say, it moved me a lot.

— I've been doing EMDR for a year. I had never reached this point. I really do it, online, I keep doing it. My therapist doesn't do Brainspotting, but I had never reached this. I've done pain protocols, but I hadn't accessed this. I hadn't talked to that child, or that aunt. I hadn't understood.

— I'm the eldest daughter of immigrant parents, shared the therapist. And I'm the oldest of four siblings! Foreign country, foreign language... We take care of so many things, so many children, so many people. There are good things that come with that, yes. We learn to respond to what needs to be done. But there's a price. And what moved me... is that no one saw your pain when you lost that aunt. Everyone saw the children's pain. But yours, no. Today we saw it. That was the injury.

— Yes.

— It was your grief. I think this is the medal of honor. I'm sure that one day — each according to their belief — when you meet your aunt, you'll be able to say: "Look, here they are. I did my best. Here are your children. I took care of them as if they were mine, with all the love you would have given. But I want you to know one thing, aunt: I missed you."

— Yes... I said that to her.

— "I did this for you. Because I love you. Love heals. Love endures. Love..." with the magic potion.

— Yes. It's a magic potion.

— Now you'll need a convalescence period. Recover slowly. Learn to live without carrying other people's bags. Learn to say no. Those bags aren't yours.

— Exactly.

— You don't need to sacrifice yourself to take care of others anymore. You had to do that. And there's no reproach in it. You did the right thing. I'm sure many people are grateful to you for it. Mission accomplished. Mission complete. "Excuse me: now I will take care of my life. Now I will take care of what is mine. My body. What I haven't lived. The things I need. I did my job very well and it's delivered. Now it's my life I need to take care of. My body, my heart, my injuries. Because it came at a high price."

— I'm at peace now. — Marta looked genuinely calm.

Now everything could be done in peace. Everything that needed to be done before, had been done. Now it was a different phase.

— Now it's time to schedule. Time to charge fairly, because otherwise we don't pay the bills. Now it's time to help when we choose to help, when we have rules for it. We're not going to be bad in old age, right? Saying "no" isn't being bad. It's protecting yourself. Taking care of yourself. Preparing for aging. If you don't fix this would today, in twenty years you'll be stiff.

— Yes. This experience made me an amazing mother. — Now Marta could see her own merit. — I have two children. I absolutely love them. And today I am certain of that.

— And certainly, it also made you a very good therapist.

— Yes. I know that too.

— I believe it. But a thirteen-year-old girl shouldn't have to do this. A thirteen-year-old girl isn't a mother. She shouldn't carry bags, take care of patients, charge fees, or do accounting. She should play in the schoolyard, have crushes on the boys.

— Yes.

— So, let's give her a break.

— Relief... Oh, wow... You know when you want to take a deep breath? — Marta inhaled again — What a relief...

— There was so much weight on your shoulders. So many responsibilities. Many years, many kilos on your back. You're going to sleep like a rock — she laughed. — I want to thank you. Your work was beautiful. Thank you for trusting me to share it.

— I thank you! I was just very worried about the time. I was tense at the beginning. I was anxious. At one point I thought: "Wow, it's so much..."

— You're thirteen. I'm the teacher. I'm the adult. I take care of those things — Esly said with a smile.

— Alright. Thank you. That was exactly it. — She smiled at the "scolding."

— When you're a therapist, you'll take care of your patients. Right now, I take care of mine. I have my own watch here. I manage my time well. I've been doing this for forty years.

— I know. But look at me, "oh my God, I'm wasting time, I'll mess up, I'm talking too much" — she exhaled deeply — but then it passed. I understood everything. Thank you so much.

Chapter 8

The Voice of Prudence

Saul took a deep breath before beginning. He was trying to organize his thoughts, speaking with some difficulty.

— Do you remember I worked with Peter on the "dangerous world" issue?

The therapist nodded, listening attentively.

— So, I accessed a chain of memories related to that, the idea of a dangerous world. Since then, I've been having recurring sensations that I'm going to be robbed.

He paused briefly.

— This isn't a new kind of dream. It's a dream I've had before.

As he spoke, Saul showed a discomfort that went beyond words. He continued:

— These dreams are closely related to an event that happened to me... traumatic, in 2006, when I suffered a "good night, Cinderella" incident during a trip. [Note: A drug often used illegally to put someone to sleep in such a way that they cannot awake while they are being sexually abused.]

He inhaled deeply, recalling the memory.

— I traveled to do a course. And I ended up going through this... "good night, Cinderella" episode.

The therapist gently interjected:

— Yes, that's fine. Are there things from that experience that you remember? Or very little?

— I remember, but actually... the bigger trauma for me was the aftermath. Because I blacked out.

He repeated, emphasizing the words:

— I blacked out. And during that blackout, in the hotel, I slept more than twelve hours. When I woke up... I woke up in a very horrible situation.

— That's enough — the therapist said. — That's sufficient. Let's go.

The therapist inquired:

— Shall we work on the hotel situation? Or shall we work on the dreams?

Saul paused to reflect before answering.

— That's a good question... Because I think the dream... Well, it's actually cause and effect.

He began describing the effects of the experience in his daily life.

— I've been having insomnia problems. Quite a bit of bruxism while sleeping. But when you go through an experience like that, I think... insomnia, bruxism, all these things are consequences of anxiety. Which is the feeling of being in danger.

— Yes — the therapist confirmed.

— So, insomnia, for me, is generally not the problem. It's the fever.

Saul used a metaphor to explain:

— When you have a fever, the fever isn't the problem. A very high fever is a problem because you need to lower it so you don't cook your brain... But the fever itself isn't the main issue. The question is: what caused the fever?

— Yes.

— Why the fever? Why a high fever, a low fever? What's the root? Is it meningitis? Dengue? Malaria? The flu, a virus? Is it something serious, something simple or complicated? The fever reveals it. It signals: there's something here you need to check.

The therapist nodded, allowing him to continue.

— So, it's the same with insomnia, bruxism...

— Yes. — She then returned to an important point. — And the dream about being robbed?

— It's the dream of feeling victimized. A situation of danger. It's what I went through.

— Yes — she said, firmly and empathetically. — I think we need to work on that situation from back then. But we don't need the details, okay?

— Great — he nodded.

— You're an adult now, right?

— I am.

— Do you have a good "endurance gauge"?

Saul chuckled lightly.

— I do.

— So, since this happened to you as an adult, no child involved, you only need to share the minimum I need to know to follow you. No need to expose lots of details.

— That's fine. Also, because... well. — He fell silent, embarrassed, his face tensing.

The therapist then asked:

— When you think about all of that, have you ever worked on it before?

— Yes.

— Great. With EMDR? With Brainspotting?

— No. I worked on it right when it happened. I was in Bioenergetics training. That was in 2006. But I've never done EMDR or Brainspotting.

The therapist straightened her posture, as if preparing both the internal and external space for the dive.

— The day has arrived. Shall we?

— Let's go.

— So, I want you to think about that and cover one eye. Let's see...

— Can I use glasses?

— No, first with your hand. Let's see.

She watched Saul attentively.

— When you think about that, zero to ten?

— With this eye... five.

— Now try with the other eye.

Saul switched and took a few seconds to process.

— More activated. I think it would be an eight.

— Do you want to work with the eight-eye, or should we go with the five-eye?

— Let's go with the eight-eye.

— Is it strong?

— Let's do it! — Saul replied, energized.

She instructed him calmly:

— So put on your glasses so the eight-eye is exposed. You know I'm here, you can see me. Anything that comes up... we'll handle it together.

She picked up the pointer.

— Let's use my pointer.

Adjusting the camera, she faced him:

— Now, think about that. What bothers you most? Where does it activate the most? Here...

She searched for the sensitive spot with the tip of the pointer. He slowly looked for the point with his eyes, as if seeking a memory in space. His focus shifted back and forth, hesitated, lingered.

— Is it okay on that side?

— Yes.

— Here?

— Here in the middle.

He moved his eyes slightly.

— I'll go a bit further... here.

— Other side.

— Down.

— Here.

— Here exactly?

— Yes.

— Let me settle myself in my chair. Now check your body. Where do you feel this?

He took a moment to respond.

— I feel a freezing.

Gradually, the images began to emerge.

— So, we're here. You're not alone.

— Yes.

— That's over, but...it was bad, it was really bad.

— It was. Now think about it... and let whatever happens happen. Let's see what comes up. This will carry you.

Pause. His body responded before words.

— I immediately feel tension here.

His gaze fixed, a scene almost as if it were present returned.

— It's like I see the spot, the reddish one, and the peripheral vision blurs...

— Out of focus.

— Exactly.

He took a deep breath.

— And when I think about that... about the experience I had...

— Has anything changed?

— It's very sensory. Because this is the memory I can access.

He was silent for a moment, eyes fixed on the spot

— And the feeling of helplessness I experienced afterward comes very strongly. I think this, deep down, is the most traumatic part.

Because when I woke up, I received no support from the hotel staff. No empathy, no one cared about what happened.

His voice trembled.

— They... didn't give me any support. None. It was awful.

— No one wanted to get involved. — Esly added.

— Exactly. No one wanted to be involved in it. No one even helped me go to the police station. Or to provide the security cameras. Nothing.

A heavy silence.

— That, for me, was... I think it was the worst part of the whole story.

He touched the base of his skull.

— When I talk about it, tension comes up here. Right at the base of my skull.

— If that tension could speak, what would it tell you?

Saul paused for a long time. An internal conflict seemed to emerge.

— Wow... the first thing that came to me was... it's even hard to say... an inner argument arose.

— It's okay if you don't want to say it.

— The first thing is... "This is your fault." And then after came... "Wait, no, it's not your fault." But the first thing that came was... "This is your fault."

— He took a deeper breath, as if wrestling with a deep and old wound.

— That was exactly the experience I went through there... a lack of empathy, it felt like... that was the message people wanted to send me. "It's your problem. You asked for this."... "You were naive, stupid, an idiot. Deal with it. We have nothing to do with this. We won't get involved. It's your problem."

Once again, he repeated it in a low, trembling voice:

— That was the most traumatic part, you know?

The silence stretched from the Earth to the Moon, bringing with it the tears of that latent memory.

— And then, when I went to the police station, I was still under the effect of drug. I couldn't tell the story properly. The police report... it was very vague. Because the people at the station didn't offer any kind of support either. — Saul was visibly struggling to breathe. — And during the 16 hours I slept, the criminals ran wild with my credit card. I ended up with a huge debt that bothered me a lot, for a long time. And the banks didn't handle it as they should have.

He took a needed pause.

— At the same time, another thing comes to mind: amidst all of that, there was an inner strength that managed to go to the police station alone, even in the chaos. That managed to change my return flight. Instead of going home, I went to my parents' house, because it was a very difficult experience. And my parents were very supportive.

— Then feel that support from your parents.

He nodded, eyes brimming with tears.

— I had the strength to say to both my sister and my mother... Because they said, "Ah, but you were very naive..." And I had the strength at that moment to say: "Look, that doesn't help me. Judging me doesn't help me." When I said that, they understood. And they really managed to support me.

A faint smile emerged among the tears.

— It's funny, because I'm working on the left eye, but the tear is running from the right, which is covered.

— Seems like the other eye knows how to cry. — The therapist commented empathetically.

— When I talk about this, the freezing starts to lessen. — He breathed more freely.

The therapist noted:

— I think anyone who goes through something like this... our tendency is to regress. We become children again. So, in a way, it was your child self that sought help from the hotel staff, that sought help at the police station. And they looked at this adult and dismissed him. But your adult self was there. In terms of inner strength. But the one in total panic was the child returning to the parents' house. I think you did very well. And the adult did very well to say: "This doesn't help me. Want to support me? Then support me. But don't judge me."

— Yes.

— And they were able to support you. It awakened compassion. Love.

— I'm floating between three things… When you brought up the child, I floated to situations where I was also hurt as a child, and left helpless. I floated to the scene. And then to the present, where in many situations I still go out in the street fearing being robbed, having my things taken. Past, present, future.

— Very well. Yes, it's all in the same package, the same bundle. So, let's go step by step. How old is that helpless boy?

— Nine.

— And the person who went through that in 2006?

— Twenty-six.

— And today?

— Forty-four.

— Can you see all three?

— Yes.

— How are they?

Saul hesitated, as if searching for the answer on their faces.

— The child is fine. The 26-year-old… still hurts. And the 44-year-old is trying… giving himself the opportunity to try… you know… to free himself from this. Because it's been so long.

His voice faltered, tired.

— I've cleaned up so much. I've sorted out so much of the mess left regarding this story. — He exhaled. — I talk about it ,and it keeps decreasing: it was at an eight, then six, now I'm at four.

The presence of the nine-year-old still lingered.

— That boy… what is he telling us by being here? Even if he's okay. — Esly asked.

The answer came slowly, like someone carefully gathering memories:

— What he says is: I was very defenseless, indeed. And his journey is to learn to defend himself a bit better.

— How can we help this boy defend himself better? Protect himself, know how to defend himself...

Esly asked after a pause, respecting the silence.

— I think he needs to learn to fight a little more. He had a purity... a purity bordering on naiveté. That's why he was very vulnerable.

— He has an inner strength that knows how to guide him.

The therapist wanted to tell a story, asked for permission:

— Jesus said that people shouldn't harm children, because children have angels, an angel that protects them and walks with them. Does that image interest you?

They smiled.

— That interests me. As you were talking, I got in touch with my grandmother.

The memory reintegrated itself, warm and full of affection.

— Both grandmothers were very religious women. Catholic, loving, caring. I have many good memories of my relationship with them. When you spoke, I got the image of my grandmother saying that. And I think, if that child could be with her, she would have definitely welcomed him.

She didn't hesitate:

— Let's take him there. Let's take this boy to his grandmother. Like science fiction, where we freeze time. Stop everything. Let's leave him there, in his grandmother's lap.

There was a long silence as he kept his gaze on the spot. Until he smiled.

— He's happy.

— Is he protected? Defended?

— Yes. Very much so! Both grandmothers are there. He's very safe.

— You even have a grandmother to choose from, wow! — The therapist added with a smile.

— Yes! They were very dear grandmothers. And he was safe in their laps.

In the end, the invitation came:

— Now see inside your body where you want to store this feeling. Forever. And be able to access it whenever you want, invited the therapist.

When he began speaking about the grandmothers, a calmness appeared in his chest that had been tight and anxious until then. It felt good to imagine. Saul remembered his childhood, the visits to the countryside where his grandmothers lived. There was no fear there. He could walk the streets, play with other children. The experience was completely different: more freedom, more respect, more care.

— I felt free. I could walk down the street without fear.

The memories came filled with light, as if that time could still be accessed.

— It's important to have this child who could walk in the streets, play, do many things, and be welcomed by these grandmothers without fear, without aggression.

At home there had never been violence, he said. But socially, yes.

— Socially, I experienced a lot.

That's why the memory of being able to exist in that collective space, without fear, was valuable. Playing, running around the city, riding bikes with cousins and friends—all of that was possible at the grandmothers' houses. It was a good image to keep.

— Bring that child who could play in the streets... without fear. — Saul relived this sweet memory.

— And if someone touched that boy? What would the grandmothers do?

— I don't know. I don't have any memory right now of such a situation near them.

— I ask because often inside grandmothers there are lionesses. As there are inside of mothers, too. "Touch my child and see what happens." This strength was what this boy needed to access now. You had already said: "this boy needs to learn to defend himself." He needs to stop being so weak, so naive... Have at least a drop of astuteness and cunning. Nothing extreme, but enough to stay alert. How to do that? Think. Look at my pointer here and think about that.

— The image that came wasn't of the women, but the men in the family. If I think of a reparative image... it would be imagining my father, my grandfathers. Teaching me, giving me more strength in this sense. I imagine my father, my grandfathers, calling me aside: "Come here, little boy. Let's arm you. teach you to defend yourself."

They were beside him, helping him defend himself. If anyone messed with him, they would be there.

— A nine-year-old boy needs someone to protect him. — The therapist added — And he also learns to protect and defend himself, with the adults defending him.

— Exactly!

This image stayed.

The therapist then shared that her father used to say not to start fights. But if I got into one, I shouldn't get beaten up. I should react and protect myself.

— You don't start fights with anyone., my dad would say. But if you're in one, don't get beaten up — fight back and fight well!

It was direct teaching, almost a commandment from someone who knew life's harshness. She laughed remembering her father's expression.

— My father was a gaúcho [a Brazilian cowboy from the south] who said he'd give a bull to not to enter a fight, but he'd give a herd not to leave it once he got in one. This code of honor marked him. You didn't provoke trouble for nothing, but if the situation demanded, you had to fight.

133

—Saul, you don't start the fight, but if you need to fight, go all in, make it count. "Now, that it's happened... let's fight for real." How much does this boy believe he can really fight, defend himself, if necessary?

— Bringing up this image, I think he believes it now.

— Is he learning?

— Yes.

— He's only nine, right? He has time to learn. But he needs to start. — She emphasized. She asked that this strength stay with him. That this capacity to learn to defend himself be inherited from his father and grandfathers, who were now there, inside him. As allies, internal figures of strength, power, and protection. — Now take all this capacity for defense and protection, and let's go to 26-year-old Saul.

An image appeared. The child said to the older Saul:

— "It's okay." But what came up very strongly was that this happened because I had low self-esteem. There were signs that danger might happen... but I didn't want to see them.

It was as if the child, now wiser, spoke to the man:

— "Trust your instincts more. Trust them more!" At the time, I didn't realize why I was consumed by insecurity. The 26-year-old Saul couldn't see why there was a low self-esteem issue there. He just didn't want to pay attention.

— He wants you to look at yourself and find the voice of prudence that, that day, you turned a deaf ear to it.

— Yes. — That voice was still inside him.

With that recognition, something began to dissolve.

— And when I get in touch with that, the activation lowers even more. — Saul observed himself closely.

His body calmed. But a small discomfort still persisted.

— The only thing that still bothers me a little... is the tension. The freezing is gone. But this tension radiates here. — He said, pointing to the nape of his neck.

— That tension still accuses you. It says: "You are guilty."

— Uh-huh.

Something different was proposed. Imaginative, symbolic, but with the potential to reorganize the experience.

— I'm going to make you another proposal. You can say no if you don't want to.

— Okay.

There was a whole group gathered. Students from the Brainspotting course were observing the session, with their cameras closed. Some important characters were ready to act.

— I spoke with the group here. You know there's a bunch of men in this group, right?

— Yes.

— And there's a lioness that lives inside many women too, you know?

The proposal was bold: symbolically go back to the hotel, accompanied.

— I propose that they go back with you to the hotel. Do everything you wanted to do at the time... everything 26-year-old in you wanted to do. They will go with you. You can fight. You can swear. We can imagine that. Is that interesting to you?

He hesitated. Something was activated.

— When you say that, it activates a little more... Because then it enters a bigger confrontation... it even gives some spasms.

It was a lot of contained energy. A lot of repressed material. But he wouldn't be alone.

— I called your grandfathers. They said they're in. I called your father, he said he'll go too. I spoke to the guys here, they all said: "We're going to defend Saul. Don't know how to fight? We'll teach you how." How does a grown-up fight? How do men do it?

The mission was set. The support was there.

— They agreed. Now it's up to you.

Something in his body still reacted. An internal effort to cross an emotional barrier.

— I'm trying to get a little past it...

It was easier to speak when the camera was off. When there wasn't the gaze of another.

— It's something... I'm going to talk to you, and everyone has their camera off. It seems like it's just you and me here, for safety.

— But they won't appear, right? It's just for me and you.

It wasn't literal, it was symbolic.

— I'm just saying that, in your imagination, we're going as a tribe to the hotel.

— Ah, okay. It's just... I felt... a little ashamed.

— You know, living this, as a situation like what you went through... I think anyone would feel this way, some embarrassment.

— Yes.

The tension concentrated in the back of his body, like he was carrying relentless judgment. The therapist helped him understand the internal voice that harshly reprimanded him:

— "Boy, you didn't pay attention to your prudence. If you had listened, you wouldn't be in this mess." But there's also another part, more indignant than guilty, that protests: "Screw you, because I didn't ask to go through this. I don't have a crystal ball! This could have happened to anyone. I didn't deserve to be treated like I was. I didn't deserve that." — Saul still felt it strongly.

— Shall we go fight? — Esly asked, encouraging him to accept the imaginary support and reframe the situation, in a version where he could defend himself and also receive support.

— Let's go — he replied, taking on the scene with conviction.

He visualized his "tribe" gathered around him. An internal noise, like drums, announced that they were all there, ready.

— The whole tribe is there, ready, everyone really wants to protect and defend you. "No! You don't do this to my friend."

It was as if, finally, someone was saying what he had never heard at the time: that it wasn't fair. That there had to be justice. She continued to encourage his imagination:

— Your friends are going to tear this hotel apart! They'll fight the staff for you: "You have to help, call the police, file a report... this happened here!"

He went silent for a moment, feeling the impact of her words.

— Wow... this is so deep... — the phrase hung in the air, tears coming. — I hadn't realized how deep this is.

He realized it was as if the emotional releases were returning, similar to what he had experienced in sessions with another therapist.

— That's okay, I'm not scared — the therapist consented.

Saul recalled the desire he had had to move a lawsuit against the hotel. But with the lack of support and imprecise records, the lawyers had told him it wasn't worth it...

— Even at the beginning, I didn't have support. The police report was very vague, and the lawyers I consulted said it wasn't worth it. I had no proof.

His body reacted to the memory. An internal, visceral burning.

— They still told me I had to thank God I wasn't killed — he said, distressed. — Because if I had woken up, they would have killed me.

And he realized that now, it wasn't an exaggeration. It was a real possibility. A real vulnerability he faced alone.

— Wow, this is very visceral. The whole digestive tract... everything burns inside, really stirring the intestines.

He then shared an association spontaneously:

— I dissociated. Because at the time, to even get to the police station under the effect of the tranquilizer—which was strong... I still had to go. You know when you feel like you've been in an accident, but you have to survive no matter what?

The dissociation he had lived through in that situation now reconstituted clearly.

— I dissociated deeply there, in the absence of people. And it seems that now... now it's like it's happening again. — Saul allowed silence to fill the space. Several minutes followed.

— Do you want our tribe to go with you to the police station?

— Ah, they're here — he replied, with a smile. — I feel them with me. It's like now I can tell the world: "This is happening to me."

Another long silence came, followed by relief.

— It's passing.

Then two thoughts came like flashes.

— What goes around comes around. And I had this fantasy that the hotel went bankrupt.

He never looked to see if the hotel still existed. But he allowed himself to imagine.

— With the pandemic...

— They really deserved to go bankrupt, for the lack of care they had. If it happened to me, it could have happened to others too. Easily. — He concluded.

Esly invited him to listen to the voice of prudence. What would it say to 26-year-old Saul?

— You don't have to go through this. Never again. — Saul said convincingly.

— Just be prudent.

— Yes. And stay alert. Everything will be fine. Take it as a lesson. Let it go.

— Yes. Let it go... — Esly encouraged.

And he did. One by one, the residues of pain, anger, guilt, and shame were released.

— I just had a thought... the world really has these dangers. The point is to stay aware of them.

— Exactly. Don't let your guard down. — Esly said, smiling.

He then concluded, with the wisdom he could now access:

— I think 44-year-old me can already see this in a more mature way...

— That's it — the therapist added. — I was going to bring all these people to talk with 44-year-old you.

— Yes. 44-year-old me can see it better. Much better.

He remained silent for a few moments, eyes still fixed on the pointer. Esly asked:

— What is he seeing?

The therapist followed carefully, respecting the time each answer emerged. She continued, now firmer:

— Do you really need to stay awake at night to make sure you won't be robbed?

— No — he replied, almost in a whisper.

— Is sleeping dangerous? — she asked, testing the weight of the memory.

— No... — he reflected, then added — Sleeping is restorative. Sleeping is great. Sleeping is wonderful. Sleeping is very good.

— Sleeping is only dangerous when someone gives you something like a "Knockout Drink".

— Yes — Saul nodded, as if seeing the scene through the prudence of today.

— So, we need prudence to avoid putting ourselves in vulnerable situations.

— Yes. And since then? Never again. I've stayed alert. — Saul stated.

There was firmness in his voice now.

— Now you hear the voice of prudence. — The therapist confirmed.

Silence settled again, as if he were reorganizing everything inside. He breathed deeply.

— Today I can... — he began, still with his eyes fixed on the pointer. — All the repercussions of that financial story... are over. Over. Gone.

— You overcame it?

— Yes.

His body seemed more relaxed, his expression lighter.

— I'm much better — he said, and the following silence was peaceful.

The therapist prompted with a direct question:

— From zero to ten?

— Regarding the freezing... — he gestured with his hand, as if measuring a drop. — I still have a tiny bit... of bodily tension. But very little. Almost zero.

And then, as if sensing something in his body:

— When I get in touch with this small tension... a word comes to me. I think I suffered. Actually... it's a matter of homophobia itself.

The next words came in waves. He paused, breathed, looked inward.

— The issue of homophobic violence... And regarding this story here... okay. But you know what comes to me? It's as if... this tension that's here... is a kind of adaptive memory. You know that idea of "adaptive one," from EMDR?

— Yes — the therapist confirmed, letting him continue.

— Like... I can't be at zero regarding homophobia. Because being at zero is being defenseless again... for a possible homophobic attack that could happen.

— That's the voice of prudence. You don't need to have tension to protect yourself. But you do need prudence. Do you understand the difference?

— I understand. — Saul confirmed.

— Because these things can happen. No one has everything under control. Accidents happen. A plane crashes. A car crashes, goes out of control. The world isn't an easy place. It's like this. "Never again," you can't promise that. But staying alert, that you can do. You need to stay alert — she reaffirmed, with conviction. — This won't zero out, because this isn't activation. That's prudence.

— Yes... yes, totally!

She invited him to return his gaze to the pointer:

— So, look at my pointer and follow it. — She moved the pointer backward, farther away.

He obeyed. When she closed the pointer, and ended the procedure, he removed the glasses.

— Cover the other eye with your hand. Now, when you think about all of that... how is it?

— Only "calm" comes... That's it. There's a tiny tremor in the eye. You know when you're a little stressed and an involuntary tremor happens? But, in principle, I don't relate it. Zero discomfort.

— And the voice of prudence lives in that eye, too?

— Yes. — Saul reflected. — Because this was the eye that got emotional the most during the whole process. It was the one that teared up...

He breathed deeply, nodding.

— I'm okay.

— What are you taking home from all this?

He thought for a few seconds, then spoke firmly:

— I take that... the strongest message that comes to me is that I made it. It was very difficult. It was horrible. But it's over. Just as I received so little support, which was very traumatic for me, I went after the support where I needed it. Within my family.

And he continued, now with a calmer smile:

— Afterwards, people were very loving with me. I received a lot, a lot of affection. A lot of support. I have this child within me who can seek the grandmothers, can seek people who embrace and say: "It's all right." He can seek the grandfathers, the father, and say, you know?

He made a final pause, as if closing a cycle:

— I lived the trauma. But I have strength. I am strong.

— And the trauma passed. The strength remained. That's what matters.

— That's what matters. — He confirmed, confident.

141

Part 4

Brainspotting Sessions Z-Axis

Chapter 9

Susana Lifts the Weight Off Her Back

Susana hesitated for a moment, as if organizing her thoughts, then said:

— Esly, today I need to work on the pain in my back. It's stronger in the lower right lumbar region and spreads across my back... like an electric current. Sometimes it reaches the cervical area, even the jaw. I have reflux. The stomach is affected too. It gets tense, painful, under the ribs.

She described with clarity and rich detail the complexity of what she was feeling. She explained that she avoided medication so as to not aggravate her stomach and had been relying on osteopathy to reorganize her body.

— Sometimes I feel like I'm falling apart...

The therapist listened attentively and asked:

— Since when have you been feeling like this?

— The worst crisis was about three years ago, but I had felt pain before. Since I was eighteen, I had a lot of tension in my shoulders. Massaging helped... but four years ago, it began affecting my lower back, until in 2016 I was completely immobilized. I couldn't get out of bed. The pain kept me from doing anything.

Susana recounted the profound impact this pain had on her life and how she sought treatment until finding some relief through osteopathy, dietary changes, and EMDR.

— What do you attribute all this to? — asked the therapist.

— I think it's the responsibility I assumed early on... When I was eighteen, my mother had another baby — a surprise. My father was ill, with heart problems, and the doctor said he only had about six years to live. My mother was desperate... so I helped out. I cared for my younger brother, took responsibility alongside her to keep things going.

She explained that she had another middle brother, seven years younger than her, and the youngest, nineteen years younger.

Noticing a reaction, the therapist observed:

— You flushed when you mentioned that you're nineteen years older than your youngest brother.

Susana confirmed, quickly identifying the source of discomfort:

— This story affects me. I get anxious, tense. The redness comes from that... I feel it in my chest, as if something stirs inside.

— When you look there... what do you see? — Esly asked gently.

— I see myself taking on something that wasn't mine. I wanted to study, but I ended up taking on a responsibility I didn't want. When I got married, at twenty-five, I thought, "Now I can take care of my life." But that didn't happen. I kept doing things for others.

The therapist proposed finding the exact point in her inner window where all this still resonated. She asked about the intensity of the discomfort:

— From zero to ten, how is it now?

— Seven — Susana replied.

With the pointer in hand, the therapist invited Susana to locate the spot. They tested positions: right, center, left. Finally, Susana pointed:

— Over there... the first point.

The therapist refined the search:

— And higher, middle, or lower?

— I think higher.

She adjusted the pointer until Susana said:

— Here. Something's coming... I have a lump in my throat, I want to cry.

— Zero to ten?

— An eight.

They had found the brainspot. The process began.

— Stay there a little bit and let's see what comes up?

Susana fixed her gaze on the identified spot. Silence stretched for a few seconds, then she began to speak:

— I think I had to be half-mother, half-father to my siblings... My mother was very fragile with my father's illness... At any moment he could die. And then? What would become of that little boy?

As she spoke, her memories came vividly, intertwined with bodily sensations:

— He was born somewhat sickly, you know? And I remember the nights, the early mornings, when I had to get up, take the car, and rush my mother to the hospital. He couldn't breathe. She didn't want to bother my father... so she called me. It was always me.

She breathed more deeply, drawing the memories in with each breath.

— At that time, my middle brother was a teenager, going out a lot, partying... And I was the one chasing him at night too, because my mother asked me to do that.

The therapist suggested:

— Look through that spot, at the wall, in that same direction. Thinking about all of this and looking there, how's the intensity from zero to ten?

— Still around an eight... but it's different from the front spot. This one further away brings some calm, it's an eight, but different. I don't have as many bodily sensations. The front point makes my heart race.

147

— A calmer eight, then.

— Uh-huh... And now nothing else comes up.

— Back to the pointer, please.

Susana subtly moved her eyes, reconnecting with the original focus. New images arrived shortly:

— What comes now is that on Mother's Day, my two brothers send me greetings. These days I even scolded one of them for never saying "I love you" to our mother, but he always says it to me.

Susana hesitated a little, then continued.

— That middle brother... I took care of him from when he was very young. When he was three, I was ten. Our mother would go to work, and I would stay with him. It wasn't a bad experience caring for him, but I didn't know what to do. I remember that sometimes he wouldn't obey, and I would lock him in the bathroom. He jokes about it today, but I know it hurt him. I blamed myself a lot for that...

— Have you asked for his forgiveness?

— I have.

— That's good.

— When I think about the pain, the word that comes to mind is "excess." Too much of everything. And I couldn't handle organizing it all. Running the household, my mother working, me studying... It was too much.

— Now look at the distant point, said the therapist.

— It's less now... A five already. Funny, it doesn't bring up new memories, and the body sensation is diminishing. Much lighter.

— And when you look at the pointer, what is it now?

— Around a four. I feel how much I still struggle with excess. When something deviates from what I planned, I get destabilized. My heart races, I blush, especially in the neck. It feels like I can't handle it, that it's too much. I get very tense, wound up.

— That was too much back then, right? — Esly said empathetically.

Susana nodded, and as if a new door opened inside her, she revealed:

— Now the memory of the accident I had comes up. I got home and said nothing to my parents.

Her voice changed tone, lower, almost secretive.

— I was with some friends. The car flipped over. I managed to get out through the back window. I got up, saw my friend, a girl I knew, nearby... I asked for a ride to the city center. From there, I walked home. Two hours. I went to a friend's house, washed my blood-stained shirt, put it back on, and went home. When I arrived, my mother was caring for the baby. My father was in the living room. I went straight to my room. I just thought: "I can't disturb them. If Dad finds out, he might die. Mom is with the newborn. I have to endure this alone."

The therapist, with empathy, completed the thought:

— And without anyone to care for you.

— The next day, I went to work. I had a cut on my face. At work, they asked.me about it I made up some story. But since it was a small town, my mother eventually found out. She came to talk to me. She asked me to tell my father.

Susana breathed deeply again.

— I did. I sat on his lap. I told him everything. It felt so good to be able to tell him. To have that lap. I didn't have that kind of open channel to talk directly to my father. Everything was through my mother. I miss that so much. He passed away, and we never truly shared moments like that.

The therapist, sensing the emotional portal opening, suggested:

— You know, I think our brainspots are kind of magical, right? We can do things in them that we normally couldn't. Don't you want to have this time with your father? Let's call him here, wherever he is, so you can have this opportunity. Say whatever you wanted to say, do what you couldn't... In your imagination, just for you. What do you think?

— I think that's great.

Susana allowed herself to dive into the picture forming before her. The space between her and the point was now fertile ground for what still needed to be seen, felt, and released.

— Take your time here, let's do this your way.

She breathed deeply. The images began to emerge gently. A silent, powerful reunion.

— I only see myself asking forgiveness and him smiling at me. My father wasn't one to scold, and he was always very easygoing… I never got a spanking from him. I see him smiling, hugging me, and me asking forgiveness for the many times I judged him, for not having direct access to talk to him… and he is just smiling. Hugging and smiling.

The image was so vivid that Susana almost felt the warmth of that embrace — the same one that marked her the last time she saw him alive.

— It's very similar to the image of the last time I saw him before he passed. I got married in December 2017, and my father passed away in February 2018… In those months, I visited them often. I missed being home. One of the last times I went, I remember arriving with a strong desire to hug him… He was taking a shower, and I thought: "Wow, why is he taking so long?!" And then, when he came out, I gave him a hug Ilike 'd never given him before.

She smiled, eyes misty. The memory, now alive in her body. It was obviously very healing.

— This image is what I try to keep in my mind. It comforts me a lot. His hug and smile… the way he looked at me. It's an emotion, but a good one. Not an emotion of despair anymore. It's eased in here.

— Look at the far point.

— Wow, I feel very light. A two.

— Back to the pointer. How is it now? — Esly carefully tracked the changes in activation.

— It is very light, too. It feels like something pressing on my chest… now it's light. It's gone, you know?

— What shall we do with these "excesses"? Go to the distant point.

— What comes to mind is letting go. I really believe that my evolution, getting out of that critical period of pain, happened because I let go of a lot. I managed to return responsibility to those to whom it belonged.

She saw it clearly now. After the father's death, the mother became so fragile that Susana officially assumed the role she had held for years — that of mother to her siblings.

— After my mother became a widow, she couldn't take on her role as a mother due to the pain of grief. So, I really had to take over. Everything, they came to me for everything. And so did she — anything related to them, she called me in to handle. Until a moment came when I said to her: "Mom, it's you. You have to know. You raised me, and the other two, too. I have no children so I don't know how to do this."

A voice caught in Susana's throat, recalling the confrontation, the outburst.

— And then I started stepping out of that role. And my mom began reclaiming the role that was hers. But there's still a lot I need to let go of.

— Go back to the pointer, the nearer spot. Look at that eighteen-year-old girl. How is she doing now?

— I feel that she needs more care.

— And who's going to take care of her?

— Me.

The answer came quickly, firmly. A choice that finally seemed possible.

— I can feel it... it's crazy, because I notice the distance between the girl and the woman I am today. But in many situations, the girl shows up — with that feeling of insecurity, of being unprotected. And that's where I destabilize. Because when I maintain my adult stance, I can handle things differently.

— But when we crash like that in life... we really do destabilize, right? — Esly joked, referencing the accident Susana had described.

— Right now, it came to me… the thought: "I'm going to leave home now, I'll take care only of what's mine." That's when it all fell apart, because there was still so much to take care of. Other responsibilities. Taking on a house that was truly mine… and I felt a bit lost.

— And shortly after that, your father passed away.

— It was a lot… one departure after another. I left in December 2017, my middle brother left in January 2018, and my father passed away in February. At home were my mother and my brother, who was just seven then. And my mother, at the time, insisted… that my brother and I return home. That I leave my husband, that I separate from him to come back. And that my brother leave his girlfriend, too.

A tense silence fell. Susana's face tightened again, eyes fixed on the spot.

— It was a huge struggle. An internal struggle, because I wanted to go back to provide her some support. But it didn't feel fair to me. I could support her from afar. I didn't need to abandon the life I was beginning to build. That's what I did. I stayed in my marriage.. But it was very hard to stay firm in my decision to remain married and not return to her house. At first, I thought about going back. — She spoke, embarrassed, and fell silent again.

— Look at the far point. [Pause.] Back to the pointer. [Pause.] Look at far one. [Pause.] Now look at the pointer. — Esly guided calmly.

— Wow, I feel very light. Now what comes to me is pride. I feel proud of myself for having returned the role to the one it whom it belonged… my mother. Today I see both of my brothers doing well. The youngest is nineteen and is going to be a father. And he invited me to be the child's godmother. I'm already the godmother to my other brother's daughter as well.

There was a pause, another deep silence. Then, as if a curtain were opening in her mind, something new emerged.

— Wow, something just came to me… I've been trying to get pregnant for a while and haven't succeeded naturally. And it came to my mind: "Why would I have a child if I have already had these?" It's as if I've already done it. I don't need to anymore. I've already fulfilled my role as a mother. Wow, that's crazy. This just came to me.

— Done being a mother?

— Even though I haven't biologically had one, I've played the role plenty.

— You did what you had to, without meaning to. But you also stepped back when you needed to, right? Look at the far point. [Pause.] Now look at the closer one.

— My mother came to mind saying: "They respect you so much more than they do me." — Eyes watery again, looking fixed ahead.

— Yes. Who was the adult there? You, right. Look far. [Pause.] Look at the closer one

— It's like my mind emptied. I don't feel... I don't feel anything. — Susana whispered, tears welling in her eyes.

— Now look at the eighteen- or nineteen-year-old girl, with all the burdens she had. Look there.

— I see the image: me, totally crazy, doing everything at full speed. Super rushed to keep up.

— Does she need to keep doing that? — the therapist asked gently.

— No.

— Tell her: "Your brother is already nineteen."

— Now I feel the sensation when he told me he was going to be a father... A feeling of motherhood. Not sad about the baby, nothing like that. But I said to him: "Now it hits me that you've grown up." He's moving out, handling his own life. It's so strange to see him as an adult now. He's not that little boy anymore. Sometimes, only a situation like this makes reality hit home... Because if he hadn't become a father, I wouldn't have realized that quite this way. It was a big shock when he told me.

— Do you need to keep being mother to these boys? And to your mother?

— No! Everyone needs to take care of their own! — Susana reacted quickly.

The therapist guided the eye movements again, firm and rhythmically:

— Look at the far spot. [Pause.] Now look at the close one. [Pause.] Look at the fare one. [Pause.] Now look at the close one. [Pause.] The therapist went back and forth a few times.

The rhythm helped Susana access a new dimension. She let out a light laugh, as if realizing something that had long been obvious.

— I have to stop being my husband's mother. — She laughed at herself. — I have habits that put me in that role... I remind him of his things, of his responsibilities, not mine. He has to organize himself, but I get worried when he's late, forgets things. So, I go there and remind him. And that's also excessive, because I already have to take care of my own stuff and I wind up taking care of his as well.

The therapist responded directly:

— Who are the adults here? If you remind him, why does he need to remember?

— Yes. — She smiled again, acknowledging the truth. — I feel comfortable this way.

— With an external hard drive like you, one don't even need a planner — the therapist joked.

Susana nodded, smiling, as the therapist invited her to revisit some significant images.

— Look at the eighteen- or nineteen-year-old girl. How is she now?

— She's fine. — Susana answered calmly.

— And the accident? How does that feel now?

— It's light.

The therapist guided her deeper:

— Look at the young woman who managed to hug her father, gave him that embrace before he passed away.

She took a deep breath before responding, her voice calmer.

— It feels very peaceful, very good. It's light... my breathing is lighter, my chest is lighter, my heart is no longer racing. At first, I felt so hot, I would start turning red here, in this area. Now it's cooled off. — She lightly touched her chest, where she had previously felt the heat.

— And when you look at your siblings?

Susana paused for a moment, then answered with maturity.

— They're adults, right? It's not that I can't help them ever, but I don't need to do it for them, I don't need to worry more than they do. I can help if they ask. I don't need to offer myself constantly.

The therapist gently challenged her again:

— Do you need to continue being their mother?

Susana shook her head slowly, firm in her decision, steady at the point.

— Not at all!

— Mother to your husband?

— Not that either. — Susana remained resolute.

As she followed her internal rhythm, she remembered a phrase from her mother during childhood, a request to never trouble her father, to always spare others. She noticed how she still carried that effort, that desire not to burden anyone.

— How long will you continue like this? — the therapist pressed.

— I don't want to anymore. I really don't!

Again, the therapist guided the back-and-forth eye movement and suggested Susana reflect on what she would do with this desire.

— I want to ask for help, allow myself to be cared for. I'm trying to learn to delegate, not to do everything on my own. Sometimes, even when I was sick, I tried to handle everything, didn't show pain. Today, I express more of what I feel, and I also accept being cared for — even by my mother; I've always been the one taking care of her. — She revealed this with emotion.

She looked at the far point, then the closer, scanning her inner world as the therapist guided her.

— Take a look inside yourself. Is there room for a baby?

— There is. — She answered with a smile and tearful eyes.

— Where exactly?

She visualized it, placing her hand on her belly, her expression full of fulfillment, as if realizing a dream.

— You've already cared for so many children borne out of your heart — your siblings. Now it's time for the child in your own belly.

She smiled and confirmed:

— Now I can have my own kids.

— I like that plural — the therapist remarked, making her laugh.

— I caught myself with my hand on my belly — Susana shared, surprised.

The conversation turned to the responsibilities she had carried and how they had weighed on her body, especially her lower back, causing the pain that was now beginning to ease.

— Do you think you'll be able to handle the changes pregnancy brings?

— Yes, now I can. Before, I was afraid, worried about the weight, the changes. Now I feel my body can handle it. — She responded confidently.

She scanned her interior again, checking for weights she still carried that didn't belong to her, to release them.

— I don't have any weights that aren't mine to release; I just need to slow down at work, and I'm already organizing that.

— The excess burdens.

— Yes. I still don't know how to say "no" properly. I see patients outside office hours, even when I don't really have time, so I don't leave anyone without support. It bothers me, but I wind up giving in. — Susana confessed.

— Remember how it was caring for your father? You had to hold everything together so he wouldn't suffer. But now that duty is over. Caring for patients is very different from caring for a father, a fragile mother, or a young child. You did everything you needed to. Now you don't have to anymore. — The therapist explained.

— That's why I need to learn to say "no."

— And what's missing for that to happen?

— Setting boundaries, really. Sometimes it's 10 or 11 p.m., and patients send messages. I reply, without even thinking about it. I need to assert myself, because they have other support networks.

— Why should they, if they have you? — Esly teased.

— Yes… — Susana replied, slightly embarrassed.

— And how are you going to take care of the baby if you're seeing patients at 10 p.m.?

She smiled awkwardly, paused in silence, and then assessed her lower back.

— Pain is at a one, just a little more in the neck — Susana replied, pointing.

— Look at the far away spot.

— Yeah, I just need to organize myself and do it.

— Here, at the close point?

— It's a one.

— And far away?

— Zero.

The therapist performed the final movement with the pointer, moving it out towards the wall.

— Come back here to the pointer and keep following — she instructed, moving the tool a little deeper. — Keep following, pointer outward.

She paused briefly, observing Susana's response.

— Release the point… close your eyes — she said calmly, withdrawing the pointer. — Breathe. How do you feel now?

Susana closed her eyes, as if something inside were dissolving.

— It's amazing how it went so far back — she said, surprised. — It's like... wow, it came to mind like a movie, you know? The past leaving behind, going away... and the pain going with it. It's so crazy, going that far back. Wow... really wild.

The therapist smiled knowingly.

— That's usually how it goes. Sessions often end like this.... Just amazing.

— Yes — Susana agreed, still immersed in the sensation. — Like... it's gone.

— What have you learned from all this?

Susana took a deep breath, as if returning to her body with more clarity.

— That I need to set boundaries. I need to pay more attention to what's mine... delegate responsibilities, ask for help. Not try to do everything alone. Allow myself to be cared for... and that's not shameful. On the contrary. I need it too, right? I'm not a machine... and even machines stop.

— And really letting go. Delegating. Giving to others. "Make a hole in the nest". If we don't create the space, someone else can't occupy it. — The therapist smiled. — As long as you handle things for your husband, he won't worry about keeping a schedule. It's very good to have you to do it for him!

Susana laughed, nodding in agreement, feeling lighter now.

— It's a lot. Sometimes I notice when he asks, "Where's such and such?" "Can you find it for me?" Nowadays I do things differently. When he asks, I don't even look. I just say I didn't find it. Then he looks, and he finds it. He says, "It was here, how come didn't you see it?" — she laughed conspiratorially. — I say, "Oh my God, yeah, I missed it!" I pretend to be clueless. Before, I would go crazy looking, feeling obligated to find it. Now I can pretend to be clueless and not search.

— That's a solution. A way to handle it. — The therapist nodded. — Why would he look if you do it?

Esly paused before offering a practical suggestion:

— I think there's one more thing I'd like to suggest: to you: get another phone.

Susana responded with a resigned smile.

— Uh-huh... Let me tell you, I've already done that. But I still fall into the temptation, believe it or not? I'll have to leave that phone at the office. Not bring it home. When I leave there, it's fine to keep it on... but leave it there. Because if I bring it home... there's a message... I check, I reply. Weekend, night, after I get home... it goes far. Too far.

— Yeah, personal phone... I don't know. — the therapist said in a more personal tone. — I'm very strict about this. My personal phone is mine. For friends, husband, family. For the cousin group, for my daughter's birthday... I'm fighting to get a second phone, resisting because I don't want to manage two. But I'm reaching the point where I need it. Because I don't give mine out. And woe to anyone who share it with someone else! — the therapist laughed, amused. — My patients don't have my phone. They send messages to the work phone. My assistant passes it along to me, I listen and respond, sometimes in another language that she doesn't even understand... Tell them this, tell them that...

Susana listened attentively, absorbing the firmness in setting limits.

— Yeah... I felt that. Before, I only had one number, personal. Then I decided to get two phones. But I fell into the temptation anyway. I bring it home... check messages, reply. I have to police myself. Find a way not to fall into the temptation to pick up the phone and answer it... weekends, evenings...

— If they know they can do that... — the therapist gently interrupted.

— ...It's because I taught them they could — Susana finished, agreeing.

— Exactly!

— Another thing I learned from a dear professor: "If it's outside hours, charge double." It's amazing how a crisis can wait until Monday of a client has to pay twice as much. I count on one hand — and still have fingers left — how many times, in 40 years, I someone paid outside regular hours

Susana smiled, recognizing the recurring pattern.

— As I listen to you, it reminds me... that's exactly how I did with my siblings. With my mother. When she called me, there was no schedule. In the middle of the night, no limits, no boundaries...

— It is one thing is to do that with family, if we want. Or need to, but with a patient? They're not your child. Not family.

— I need to cut that out...

— Grab a little pair of scissors. I'll lend you mine, the therapist laughed...then softened her tone to close the session.

— Go home and think about the baby. And how you're going to create space for this baby inside you. In your relationships, in all of these that we've explored — past and present — to have a different future. Remember, if you do the same things, the results will always be the same.

— Yes — Susana agreed, expression lighter. — Thank you so much! It was wonderful. Wow... I feel like I've dropped some weight.

— You dropped a lot of weight! That's why you had so much pain. Because you were carrying many years' worth of weight. No human body can handle that.

— At some point it bursts, right?

— Your body is saying, "Oh... enough. I can't anymore!"

— Uh-huh. Exactly.

— Very good.

Chapter 10

Helena's Leaky Bag

Helena began by talking about her professional journey.

— I graduated 10 years ago — she explained, and that she has always sought to improve herself by taking various courses. However, her practice has mostly focused on volunteer work.

— I worked a lot with people with chemical dependencies and was always involved with church activities — she shared.

She had tried on several occasions, to direct her work toward private practice but felt that it hadn't worked out.

— I even started doing some private sessions, but I failed miserably — she admitted. — The people who came to me couldn't pay. They came from families with serious financial difficulties.

Despite that, Helena has a stable job:

— I have a permanent public service position. This year, I even got a managerial role, a position of trust.

Even so, she said that her work outside the public service didn't progress as she wished.

— I get wonderful feedback from the people I see; some even came because of the EMDR course that I did, because of all of the sessions to complete the training — she explained with a smile. — I didn't charge, because I was learning. Some clients stayed, but no paying clients appear. I advertise, friends refer people to me, but .. no money.

Helena spoke candidly about the barrier surrounding this issue:

— I literally have a block, and I've been working on it in therapy. I'd tried years ago, without success. I realize I have a lot of difficulty charging people. I identified several things from my childhood — she said —lack of recognition and value, not knowing how to make money. At my job, it's going okay now. But in private practice, it's not working. I hear cases, I think, "I can handle this, I can see clients," and I really can, but I don't know what happens—I can't grow professionally. I know I'm capable, I study a lot, I read a lot — she added — but something holds me back. It doesn't move forward. I don't know what else to do.

— So, you have a job that ensures you don't need the private practice, said the therapist.

— It's not that I don't need it, because honestly, that's not what I wanted to be doing with my life. I want to work as a psychologist. But I'm there because I tried private practice and it didn't work. I did other things because I had no other way to support myself, you know? And what I earn there isn't that great either.

— And if you earned from your profession, would you leave that job?

— Absolutely! This year I took the course thinking that next year I would already have some clients, enough to return to private practice and leave the job.

— So, the plan is to leave your job?

She laughed, a mix of lightness and frustration in her tone.

— Yes, honestly, I never should have taken it. I never wanted to be there.

The therapist asked her to identify where the "knot" of the whole issue was:

— How do you hold this knot? Where do you feel this block?

Helena thought for a moment:

— I don't know. In my therapeutic process, it's gone in several directions. I sought a therapist from another approach to leave my comfort zone. I want to identify what's happening. While I was with another therapist, I worked on many things, but never got close to the root or resolved this. I identified several problems related to childhood and adolescence. It was a relatively scarce environment at home, even though it wasn't exactly so.

Helena recounted how her parents were always very controlling with money, especially her mother:

— My mother was extremely controlling. We never went hungry, but if we wanted to buy new clothes, we couldn't. If there was an event, a party, I had to borrow clothes or wear something old. Buy a dress for a coming out party? Forget it! Not a chance of spending on that.

Although she didn't suffer serious deprivation, she felt the financial rigidity at home.

— My mother was always very strict in this sense, both in my childhood and later. We paid the mortgage, my parents always had a financed car, a financed home, but for us, there was no luxury. All the other kids at school had it, but not us. "You're not everyone," they would say.

Helena was attending the session by phone. The therapist asked why. She explained that she wasn't using her computer because her house had been broken into two days earlier. Her eyes immediately filled with tears, her voice trembling, still under the effect of the experience.

— They took the computers, the TV, many items... — she said, looking down, wiping her face. — I even worried afterward because I had sent a message on Friday about the session...

She admitted she was still very shaken.

— I already have nothing... and they still steal from me, right? — Esly said.

The loss was significant. Luckily, she still had her phone—the family had left the house at the time of the robbery. There was a brief silence until she resumed, almost as if opening an old journal of records.

— This is another thing I've already brought to therapy... — she recounted. — This happened many times throughout my life. Many times.

She recalled that in every home she had lived in, at some point there had been an invasion or burglary And it wasn't just domestic theft:

— I've been robbed in every possible way. On the street, by myself, coming back from college... on the bus... I won't go on... — she murmured, her eyes heavy. — It feels like I've been trying to deal with this situation since Friday, and failing.

It was still difficult to understand the logic of continuing to strive. Her doubt came out as a sigh:

— Why should I work hard, to have good things... if someone comes and steals everything I've worked so hard for?

Even so, she shared that she worked a lot. More than that, she devoted a significant part of her time to volunteer causes.

— I've volunteered everywhere. I've done a lot of volunteer work in my life, since I was a child. — Then her tone shifted to a more serious note. — I learned how to serve, to give, but not how to receive. For me, not having money isn't about laziness. It's thinking I can't, I'm not allowed... because I see what I do, and I know I do a good job, I'm dedicated. I know I'm good at what I do...

She looked sideways, as if searching for meaning in some invisible part of the room. The participants offered a full and empathic silence, many moved to tears as they listened.

— But why can't I get recognition? Why can't I earn from this?

The therapist figured it was time to find the brainspot that could access the depths of all this pain. They began exploring, slowly moving the pointer across her field of vision until they found the right place.

— Let's find our spot... — said the therapist, guiding the movements.

Helena adjusted the screen position, responding as they tested:

— There, that's good... a little more this way...

They calibrated further:

— More here in the middle… a bit higher… a bit lower…

Until she concluded:

— I think it's there, more in the middle.

The therapist suggested testing the position. Adjustments could be made if necessary.

— When you look at this spot… how much does it bother you, from zero to ten?

— Eight.

— Now I want you to look *through* this point… and tell me how much it bothers you when you look *through* it.

There was a brief silence before her response.

— Nine.

The intensity was high. The therapist offered a choice:

— Thinking about that… do you want to start with the closer point or the farther one?

— The farther one is fine — Helena replied without hesitation.

— Do you want me to hold the pointer here or can you do it without me?

— Without is fine — she answered. — I'll fix my gaze here. With the little letter there, I feel more confident to maintain the point.

Confirmed: the chosen point was the farther one, intensity nine.

— I want you to look at this point and think about this. Everything you just told me. See where you feel all this… in your body.

She stayed silent for a few seconds, then instinctively placed her hand on her abdomen:

— In my stomach. Feels like a basketball… in the pit of my stomach.

She remained quiet again, her gaze still fixed. Something opened inside. Her voice emerged, layered with memories:

— I remember when I was a child… a school I attended, I must have been four or five years old…

It was an old memory but very vivid.

— On the first day of school, I met my classmates... My mother had to go in with me that day. And there was a girl... her mother had already entered, done what she needed, and was leaving. But the girl didn't want to stay in class. She cried a lot, because she didn't want her mother to leave.

She inhaled slowly, as if feeling the atmosphere of that moment again.

— I took her hand... I told her I'd go in with her. I said, "We'll go together, you have a friend now." And I led her into the classroom.

She paused, her gaze still fixed on the point.

— And every day she would only enter the school when I arrived. She would wait for me at the door. Later she made other friends, but she still waited for me to go in. And on that first day, when I got home... my mother had already told the whole family what had happened. She was surprised.

She paused briefly before repeating, as if reliving the words clearly:

— She said I was going to be a psychologist. I didn't even know what that was yet. And whenever something happened... two friends would fight, one of them would come to me. "Come with me to talk," so I could mediate. It was so natural... people sought me out. And I was always available. I wanted to help. I wanted to...

At that moment, the therapist gently intervened to help maintain visual focus:

— Please stay on the spot as you speak, or shall I put my pointer back? Bring this spot closer... look at it.

She obeyed. Her gaze shifted to the new, closer point. A brief silence preceded the deeper dive.

— I remember my mother... — she said, almost in a whisper.

The words came punctuated by harsh memories.

— Whenever I said I needed something... like new sneakers, pants... something that was very worn... she would say: "You don't need that. You can keep using what you have. It will last a little longer." — She sighed deeply. — "It's no use buying it because you're growing. You don't need it."

Her mother's words had taken root. The therapist asked gently:

— What did you want to say to your mother in those moments? When she said that to you? You can just imagine it... you don't have to tell me if you don't want to. Just imagine.

She kept her gaze fixed on the spot and replied in a low voice:

— That I felt so embarrassed... walking around looking like a beggar in my teens. And we weren't even in that kind of financial difficulty. Not to the point of not being able to buy clothes.

Tears streamed endlessly, it was hard to keep her eyes on the spot. She paused, then continued with more firmness:

— I felt so ashamed. I saw my cousins... my uncles had much more financial difficulty than we did. And yet... they got new clothes, sneakers, things. But we didn't.

Once again, the same phrase resurfaced, heavier this time:

— I was so ashamed.

The therapist asked:

— From zero to ten, how intense is that shame now?

— Twenty! — Helena replied without hesitation.

The response came like a discharge—high, precise, undeniable. After a few moments, another memory emerged, now in a more reflective tone:

— I remember my parents saying the only thing they would do... and my mother said this millions of times in my life... — She paused, as if rediscovering an important piece of the puzzle. — I hadn't connected it before... But she said they would help us as much as they could with our education. Whenever they could, they paid for private school... But most of my life, I was on scholarships. Whenever I studied at a private school, they requested a scholarship. Because, in fact, paying for me and my sister would have been too much.

She stared intently at the point. It was far away, yet fully present in her inner self.

— She said they would pay for our studies. That it was the best they could give us. Because education, no one could take that from us. Everything else could be stolen. But our knowledge, never.

— Go back to the far spot. How is it now?

Helena obeyed, but almost immediately brought her hand to her abdomen:

— Wow, I feel really nauseated...

— For someone with a basketball in their stomach, it's even hard to breathe, right? What does this ball tell you? — the therapist asked.

— That it's heavy... suffocating.

After a few moments, the complaint turned into a heartfelt outpouring:

— What's the point of all this knowledge?

— Exactly. "If I can't even buy a dress for a coming out party, for the quinceñera? Even the computer I buy gets stolen..." — the therapist empathized.

— I study, I'm an excellent student, I've never stopped taking courses — but what's the point if I earn nothing from it? I help so many people and fall behind, we never have money for anything.

The therapist invited her to imagine a solution:

— Look at that ball in your stomach. Let's see what we can do with it.

Eyes still fixed, Helena visualized:

— I opened up my stomach, took out this ball... make a basketball with it, score some points. — She smiled.

— That's it, do it mentally — encouraged the therapist.

When silence returned, Helena whispered, dabbing her face:

— I don't want this in my life anymore.

Then came the recurring memory of burglaries and the hollow consolations she had always heard: "Rings may go, the fingers remain... at least you're okay." Helena shook her head:

— No, we're not okay, not at all! I worked hard to have something. My house was broken into, everything ransacked... so many times. There's no way to feel okay with that. And I don't want to go into debt to take expensive courses and continue only seeing patients for volunteer work.

The therapist reflected:

— To change this, you'll have to disobey your mother.

Helena furrowed her brow, still looking at the nearer spot, which now represented the focus of her pain.

— Disobeying your mother is a serious matter... What do you think? — the therapist's voice came calm. — You're going to have to take on more than just your studies. She taught you with all the best she could offer, but today you might need to choose differently.

Helena took a deep breath, keeping her eyes fixed on that point, feeling the weight — and the promise — of the possibility of new choices. The therapist guided her gently, reflecting on the roots of that stomach pain — the "basketball" — and what she was carrying. Touching on something fundamental, she commented:

— You were taught by your mother with the best she had. But maybe she has her own issues with money, right?

Helena nodded, her eyes still fixed.

— Yes, she went through a lot of need. My father too. They were hungry from childhood into adulthood. So today, I think they're still afraid of running out. They always did the best they could, better than their parents.

— That explains a lot — said the therapist — but it doesn't mean you need to continue in the same logic. Nobody is starving now. Least of all you.

After a long silence, the therapist offered a provocation:

— To have the good things in life, maybe you'll need to disobey her. Not out of rebellion... but to take a different stance on life.

Helena stayed silent for a few seconds.

— Think about it, see if it's possible — encouraged the therapist.

— It has to be... — Helena said, more to herself. — It has to be!

— It's up to you — the therapist returned. — Only you can know if it's possible or not.

And she nodded:

— Go back to the far spot. Let's see what this point will show you now.

The conversation with the therapist deepened, and Helena seemed to traverse internal layers, reflecting not only on the present but on her distant childhood. The therapist, in a calm tone, pointed out:

— Now you're over 18. You can pay your own bills. You're responsible for yourself. Your mother and father gave what they could, but they won't — and can't — support you forever.

— I know — she nodded.

— And now you'll have to negotiate with them... with this inheritance, with this obedience. If you want to, of course.

— I want to — she replied, firmly.

— Then imagine that conversation. It doesn't have to be literal. Make it your way.

Helena breathed deeply, searching for courage deep within herself.

— I wish I could have said this as a child. I wish I could have shown that... that I needed, that I deserved it. But I couldn't.

— Now you can. Now it's your chance. Go there, inside of you, as an adult, together with the child who couldn't say those things at that time.

— I can handle it — she replied. — We can handle it.

Silence. Her breathing intensified slightly, until she began to speak, her voice trembling:

— What I want to say is that knowledge isn't everything... if I don't know how to value what I know, if I can't earn anything from it... it's useless. I want a return for everything I've studied, for everything I've learned, for all the work I've done.

— It's no use learning and not making money. We learn to live, to pay the bills — the therapist agreed.

Helena breathed deeply again, as if all the air in the room wasn't enough.

— Being a good student, getting good grades... that was just the minimum. They were proud, I know. But I never felt deserving of the good things. I helped everyone everywhere and got nothing in return.

The therapist nodded compassionately.

— You obeyed your mother well. You were a good student, a good professional, a good psychologist. But now? Do you still need her permission to earn money?

Helena thought quickly, shaking her head firmly:

— No.

— It might be hard for her. But what if you explained it this way? Tell the mom inside of you that you're grateful for the knowledge they gave you, but now you also need permission — even if only internally — to be valued, to earn money, to have enough?

— I don't need to obey anymore. I can receive. I can charge for what I do. — She said this after some time.

Her gaze remained fixed on the point. The therapist suggested:

— Then bring the point close... Now look at it far away.

— Every time you tell me to look far away, I feel it in my stomach. The basketball... — she sighed — I feel it tighten.

— Bring it to the closer spot... — Esly continued the movement a few more times. — And now, how's the "basketball"?

— It's a tennis ball now.

— And do you want to live the rest of your life with a tennis ball in there?

— No! I don't want to live with any of that. No ball at all!

— I think you'll need a few surgeries then. Let's get rid of this stuff.

Endless seconds of silence, her face drenched, as if those tears would never end.

— Have you reached the point of "enough"? Have you carried this long enough, or do you want to carry this tennis ball a little longer?

— No. Enough!

— How are you going to get it out?

— I'm going to open my stomach again...

— Let's open it. Cut it open? really?

There was a pause. A deep breath for a few seconds.

— Do you see the ball?

— It's very bloody now... but it's a tennis ball. Green, with that little fuzz...

— Are you going to leave it in there? Or take it out with your hand, a clamp, an instrument?

— I took it out with my hand.

— And how's the hole where it was?

— Free.

— Free? Is there space there?

— Yes. It's clean.

— Take a moment to breathe and see if there's really room to breathe.

Helena breathed.

— See if you need to do anything else before we sew you up. You're not going to leave it open, right?

— No. It's clean. Just close it.

— Close it then — the therapist suggested gently.

— Closed.

— There might be a scar, but that's okay. What are you going to do with the tennis ball?

— I want to throw it away. Like a golf ball. Really far. I want to hit it so strongly you can't even see where it lands.

— That's your desire. You have many desires... but will you act? Will you just stay with the desire, or will you do something with it? — the therapist asked with a smile.

— I'll do it. I'm positioning it here... A perfect swing. It's gone.

— Never to come back?

— Never to come back!

— How will you keep it from coming back?

— I'm thinking about it now, it seems like it was a little marble that kept growing. I won't swallow any more little marbles. Only what I want to grow, will grow inside me.

— And what do you want to grow?

— Prosperity.

— And how do we achieve prosperity?

Helena smiles, breathing deeply.

— That's a good question.

— Go to the faraway spot again.

But just hearing the phrase "go far" made something freeze in Helena.

— What happened? — Esly noticed Helena's face contorting.

— No... it's that whenever you say "go far"... — she paused — it feels difficult... my breathing becomes hard.

It took a moment for her to continue.

— But it's already better. Before, when you said, "go far," it felt like a punch in the pit of my stomach. Now it's much less.

Still, it wasn't light at all.

— It's much less... but it's not zero.

— Helena, what's there that I haven't seen yet? — asked the therapist.

Silence. Until she named it:

— It seems like courage is missing. Every time you say, "go far," I need a lot of courage to go there.

The word "courage" opened the way to a deeper memory.

— Disobeying your mother really does require courage — the therapist reinforced.

— Especially mine — Helena sighed, resigned. — Her nickname was "General" when I was younger.

— Do you think she's reasonable enough, even being a "general," for us to talk to her and explain all this?

— Yes. I think so — Helena breathed deeply.

— Go back to the nearer point. Did you watch *The Wizard of Oz*?

— I watched it as a teenager. A long time ago.

— Remember the lion? He needed courage. The wizard is the one who gives courage. What do we have here, at this near point, that can give you the courage to talk to your mother?

— My maturity. I'm no longer a child who has to obey her. I have to make my own decisions. I have to take action, even if it contradicts what she is telling me to do.

She remembered a recent episode.

— Because this year, for the first time in my life, I had to face her in another situation. I stood my ground. I said I wouldn't accept what was happening. I had never done that before. I didn't yell at her. I didn't disrespect her. But I stood my ground. And it worked.

— It worked?

— She stopped. She listened to me. She understood. She didn't talk to me for a month. But things changed. Now she's talking to me again. Everything's fine.

Even though the bond had been shaken, the certainty was clear.

— I know that maybe the relationship will be a little shaken, but we will get past it, and there are things she needs to hear. And I need to stand my ground, regardless of what she does. I have to take my stand. — Helena finished.

— So that was it. A "sufficiently porous" mother. When something is said, she listens, takes it home, digests it. It takes time, but eventually she accepts it. Do you know what that is? Love. She loves you enough not to want to break the bond. Loves enough to think and, who knows, maybe even accept it. I'll tell you something I "saw"… and you tell me if it makes sense. If it doesn't, that's fine too.

The therapist painted a picture, suggesting Helena imagine a basketball court. At the moment she was going to make the basket, a whole basketball team appeared around her. A team. A cheering crowd.

— Go ahead, make the basket! You can do it, you can do it! They're all there with you. A fan club cheering. You know… I never had that. A team, like that, everyone together. You weren't even in the game. You were there, sitting, watching your own life pass by.

— Now, not anymore. You need to be in the game.

— Do you want this team to go with you to talk to your mother? To give you courage?

She breathed.

— I think I'd rather go alone. I just want a hug afterwards.

Done. Even if she went alone, there was a cheering crowd. A whole team rooting for her.

— It's something *I* need to do.

— You're the one who has to do it. — The therapist agreed.

She prepared herself.

— Let's do it! Go to the far point…

Silence. Breathing. Courage. After some time in silence, she announced:

— It's done! I did it! Now for the hug!

— Wonderful! And… did you hear what your mother said?

— She said: "Go. Make money." She gave me permission. And I heard it from my father too. He appeared beside her. He hugged me, too. He said: "You deserve it, daughter. Go ahead. Get rich."

Helena was still crying.

— I feel lighter. It's been a long time since I cried like this.

Her husband always said she had a heart of ice.

— But it's just for crying. Because I am generous, maybe even too much.

She gave everything. Clothes, time, energy. She had no attachment to anything material.

— I never learned to have attachment to anything.

— The burglars were going to steal the stuff anyway, right? — Esly added.

— Everything got really shaken on Friday. I was very shaken. But it felt like I was in shock, I stayed firm on the outside. I didn't even think the session would work. I wasn't prepared. Didn't even have a tissue nearby. Now my shirt is soaked. — She smiled with tears on her face, wiping them on her shirt.

She breathed deeply.

— Go far on the point. Is that okay?

— Okay.

— Breathe. Bring it near.

There were still a few minutes left. Enough time for a suggestion. The therapist spoke:

— There's a leak somewhere. I have the feeling of a purse with a hole. You earn and lose, you acquire and are robbed... what you have, you give away. A generosity... to the point of excess. Work, work, work... and the purse is leaking. You lose, in one way or another.

The therapist continued:

— Another thing that came up since the beginning of the session: this girl needs protection. You need protection. Too many robberies! Jesus said we shouldn't harm a child, because they have an angel who sees the face of God. You were a child once. So, you also have an angel, right? And this angel doesn't leave. I've never seen anywhere that you can fire him. Think about that... An angel that communicates directly with God. Think about your angel. Not just anyone. Not a decoration on a shelf. Someone trustworthy. Someone with authority. Go to them. Ask for advice. Talk to them. Tell them whatever you want.

Helena's swollen face, still soaked with tears, kept her eyes fixed on the point, in silence.

— Helena, I want you to imagine how this angel can help you. How does he fix your purse... to stop everything from leaking, to stop losing everything along the way.

After a while, and a river of tears:

— I see him sewing my purse. Literally. He stitched up the tears... and then he sat at the sewing machine. — She laughed recounting the very unlikely scene. [Pause]. — But then he got up, grabbed this half-sewn bag, and threw it in the trash. He said: "You know what? This one is old. I'll give you a new one."

New. She laughed through the tears, moved.

— Enough of that old stuff, right? Enough! — said the therapist.

And there it was:

— It's beautiful. It's huge. It's black leather.

— Lots of prosperity! I already like it.

— The old one was made of sackcloth. Of course, it ripped easily. Now it won't. I like my new purse. I've never even seen one this beautiful. It was made just for me. There's nothing like it in the world.

— And what about protection? Because it's no use having a new purse... if you can't carry it. We have to see with him how to protect it. — Esly was referring to the angel.

Even before the therapist spoke, she was already thinking:

— I was thinking... Will this new purse tear, too? Will it rip? But you know what I thought? I really liked reading Bernard Cornwell... English historian, you know? He writes medieval novels.

She remembered the descriptions of battles, the armor, the chainmail.

— I kept imagining this... The black leather purse, super beautiful. And then we started adding protection on the outside, made of metal. But then we decided: let's protect it from the inside, so the look doesn't get ruined. It will be protected like a bank safe. So strong...

that if someone tries to cut or tear it, they won't succeed. Nothing gets through.

When she finished reinforcing everything, the angel placed a hand on her shoulder and said:

— Don't worry. It's good. We'll keep it like this, but I'll carry it for you. Now you have an escort.

She smiled, still wet from the tears.

— A bodyguard? — asked the therapist.

— Yes. Definitely.

— Go to the far point and check.

She did. Come back. Checked.

— There's a bodyguard, yes. Bag protected.

She went back once more, and now something new appeared:

— A weapon... at the waist. — She laughed. — I'm armed now. I like it.

— Can I be a little naughty? Let's see... what would your mother think of all this?

— Oh, I don't care at all! — Helena replied promptly. — But I think she would be quite proud that I can save money.

With her eyes closed, she was invited to release the brainspot.

— See where you will keep all of this inside you?

She breathed deeply.

— It's here inside... inside my chest. — Hands over her thorax.

— The hands help hold it. To protect it. — The therapist worked toward closing the session.

— It's here. It's mine.

The therapist smiled.

— Very beautiful. I'm glad it's like this now.

And then she asked:

— If you came to see me five years from now, and were to tell me about your private practice, your work, the clinic... what would you say?

Helena laughed.

— The first thing I'd ask is: where are you? In Brazil? Canada? United States? Wherever you are, I'll come to you. I'll visit. By plane. First class — she laughed loudly.

— Wow! That's great!

— It's wonderful! Now I have money for that.

Chapter 11

Sight Beyond Sight!

Julie began with a wide smile and a light sigh. It was the second module of the Brainspotting workshop. She had agreed to do a session with Dr. Esly for a demonstration of the technique.

— In the last module, I worked with another Brainspotting trainer — she began, memories surfacing slowly as she spoke. — It's been basically twenty years, over twenty years, since I last played the violin. I tried twice to come back. I even entered music college... I finished almost a year. I played at weddings, taught music... But in the end, I switched to psychology.

The reason came abruptly, like a blade.

— I had an accident... I was trying to open a small bottle, without a bottle opener. I grabbed a knife to open it... — she gestured briefly, pointing to her palm as if reliving the scene. — When I applied force, the knife went into my hand.

A moment of silence. The episode still marked her.

— I needed three stitches. After that, I didn't go back. I got scared. — And in a whisper: — I stopped playing. I gave up on a musical life.

There was a moment of hesitation, as if a part of her resisted the lament that would come.

— Not even as a hobby... And it's something that would do me so much good, right? — she lifted her eyes, seeking understanding.

— Yeah, an instrument is a real companion. — Esly agreed.

— I have a violin here. — she nodded. — Closed up. Beautiful. (Julie pointed at it behind her.)

A faint melancholic smile appeared.

— But I'm always stuck in this performance anxiety. It's never good enough. I'm not playing the pieces. It's always bad, bad, bad...

And then, almost resigned:

— I don't move forward.

— Do you ever pick up the violin, Julie?

— Very few times. Throughout all these years, very few — she thought for a moment. — The last time was at the beginning of the pandemic, about two years ago. I picked it up for a few months, started studying again... but only if I'm completely alone. Like, nobody within miles.

— She laughed at her own exaggeration.

— I understand you more than you imagine. Because I come from a family of musicians. My sister has a doctorate in organ performance. She's a concertist. She also cut her hand once, while washing dishes. Broke a glass. Bad cut. — Esly explained. — But she was so lucky... She had an English student who was a doctor, a plastic surgeon who *only* operated on hands, because that was his specialty!

— Wow... what luck! — Julie commented.

— Yeah. She wrapped her hand in a towel and went to him. He stitched it perfectly. She asked how much she owed... And he said he wouldn't charge, because she would never be able to afford him. She's very talented! Ambidextrous. She wrote letters with the other hand... And continued playing. There are three of us girls. The youngest traded in the dining table for a baby grand piano...

Julie's eyes widened, a mix of amazement and disbelief.

— That's amazing!

— But she only plays for herself — the therapist added, amused. — And I also play in secret, most people don't even know I can play.

The comment seemed to open a door in Julie's thinking. She continued, like unraveling old beads:

— So... I'm terrified of needles. And there's a history... several episodes. — She breathed deeply. — At four, I cut my tongue jumping from one sofa to another at home. I needed several stitches. They held my feet, my head, stitched the tongue without anesthesia. Several stitches.

The therapist's face stayed attentive, without interruption.

— Later came a high fever, I must have been five or six. They suspected meningitis, they had to do a lumbar puncture. They put me on a table, lying like a little bean — Julie mimed the "little bean" with her hands. — They inserted the needle, took it out, inserted again, and said, "Don't move or you'll never walk again." I froze.

She swallowed hard.

— Later, I was hospitalized, with an infection that went to my kidneys. I had to take a lot of shots. Another painful prick. Result: today I can't even get blood drawn; just seeing a syringe makes me feel sick. And the last needle was the one from the violin. Three stitches in my hand, and I never went back, not even as a hobby.

The therapist shook her head with gentle reproach.

— Oh, my goodness! All that just after they said: "if you move, you'll never walk again" — she sighed. — We need to take care of these memories!

Julie nodded, exhausted but hopeful.

— So much so that today I have fibromyalgia symptoms. I've been dragging my shoes since childhood... When we start talking, the memories start coming...

— Then let's start way back — suggested the therapist, consulting her notes. — At the tongue cut, the scene when you were three to four years old. Can you see yourself there?

Julie closed her eyes for a moment.

— I remember the blood, the towel, my great-aunt's anxious voice... and the fear when she widened her eyes. I thought: "Is this serious?" What could help? Salt. We put salt on the tongue, and the bleeding didn't stop. No way, we had to go to the hospital. Small town, Sunday night. No car. Chaos.

— Okay. Let's locate a safe point to fix your gaze and work on the scene — the therapist gently guided. — Are you ready?

— Let's go — Julie responded, adjusting in the chair, taking a deep breath, willing to face the past with the bow — and the future — in her own hands.

The therapist calmly raised the pointer, guiding Julie's gaze across her field of vision.

— Take a look — she suggested. — Let's see how your body responds to each position.

Julie obeyed in silence, following with her eyes.

— Oh... the middle one — she corrected herself, after a few adjustments. — A bit higher... now lower... in the middle. There. That's it.

She settled into the chair, taking a deep breath.

— Now, when you think about that scene at four years of age... How intense is the activation, from zero to ten?

Julie reflected for a second.

— Four.

The therapist raised an eyebrow.

— Really?

— Yeah... — she murmured, thoughtful. — But it seems to fluctuate... I think it's rising to six.

— Six... increasing?

Julie nodded. The therapist then suggested:

— Look through the pointer, over there at the wall. And see what it's like there.

— There... lower. About four.

— Then stay there. Think about that whole thing... and look through the pointer.

Silence. A silence heavy as hospital air on a Sunday evening. Julie murmured, almost whispering:

— It's the same feeling... being on the table. Wanting to scream. Struggle. Like I see the little girl... wanting to shout everything she couldn't, because they couldn't anesthetize the tongue. — Julie froze for a few seconds, feeling her body respond to the bitter memory. — Even a spasm in my hand — she said, astonished. — Like my hand was reliving it!

The silence was held patiently.

— Bring your gaze closer. Here — the therapist guided. — Does anything change?

— It changes... it changes. That six isn't six anymore. Seems like that four came here.

The therapist waited a few moments, then asked:

— And how is the little girl now?

— Not so scared... but she's not calm either. She has that face like she's cried everything she had to cry... — she breathed. — After it was stitched. It hurts, but crying won't help. And she's calming down.

— Cried everything she had to cry?

— I think she's on the way. — she laughed, hopeful.

— Then look at the wall again... through the pointer.

Julie took a deep breath and followed with her eyes. Until suddenly she burst into laughter. Loud, abundant laughter.

— It changed! This is crazy! I see the heat... the speed... like in the Thundercats cartoons, "sight beyond sight" when they see far... everything accelerates, you know? At the beginning of the cartoons... they ran and ran... It's like I start to really believe. That it's okay to jump, run.

The therapist smiled gently.

— Then tell her that. You're an adult now, you understand this. Will she never play, or jump again?

— She can — Julie repeated, as if teaching herself. Maybe all she needs is to see it through that gaze, like a Thundercat. That long-range vision.

— Then bring it close here, with the pointer. And when you look at the little girl here, what happens?

Julie got emotional:

— She wants to learn to play the castanets. Like her grandmother. Not a violin… but it's even castanets, need to move the fingers — Julie added.

A new silence fell, now light.

— What's happening?

— Now it's just a body sensation, like a connection between the nape of my neck and the arms.

— Okay. Bring it close. Now far. [Pause.] Look close. [Pause.] Look far. [Pause.] And now, how is it? — asked the therapist.

— Almost zero.

— Almost?

Julie nodded.

— It's like the little girl is still scared. Like she's saying: "Don't let go of my hand, because this could come back…"

— And what would you say to her?

Julie breathed deeply.

— No. That's already in the past. Just because it happened that once doesn't mean it will happen again.

— And the tongue? — the therapist asked, with a slight smile. — Is it okay now?

Julie nodded, with a hint of irony.

— The tongue is fine… but the hands are tingling.

— Bring it close then — the therapist guided.

Julie murmured, half in disbelief, as if rediscovering her own body:

— I didn't even remember the tongue existed…

— And now?

— I think it's okay — she replied, with some doubt in her voice.

— Go to the far spot and check. Then come back close and look again.

Julie moved her gaze accordingly. She took a deep breath.

— It's the fear of letting go...

The therapist leaned in slightly:

— Why the fear of letting go?

Julie didn't respond, remaining still, inert.

The therapist suggested:

— Go back and forth. Five seconds here... five seconds there. Let's see.

After a while, Julie positioned herself.

— It's okay.

— Zero to ten?

— Zero.

— And far away?

— There... zero — and shortly after: — There is more zero on the far one than the zero up close — and she laughed.

— There it's "zero zero." Now, let's visit that little girl... the one reacting to the lumbar injection? Suggested the therapist.

Julie furrowed her brow, as if entering another scene, startled.

— How intense is it there? Zero to ten.

— She's scared. Eight.

The therapist continued:

— Look at the wall. Zero to ten?

— Eight, but gentler. Soft eight. If that makes sense... — and they laughed together.

— The four-year-old has already healed... — the therapist commented. — And what shall we do with this six-year-old, so scared? The doctor said if she moved, she'd never walk again...

Julie lifted her chin, feigning bravado:

— Pfft! I stitched my tongue without anesthesia. And here I am, talking a mile a minute! — she laughed again. — I'm over it, right?

The therapist refocused her:

— Bring it here, close.

Julie returned her gaze to the closer spot.

— It's like a 3D movie — she commented. — You get that urge to duck, even knowing it's not real. Wanting to move out of the way — Julie moved as if dodging an imaginary object.

— Then go back to the wall.

Julie was silent, deep in thought. Minutes later, the therapist asked:

— Bring it close. How does it feel now?

— I notice more body sensations.

Silence.

— And far away... How is it? — asked the therapist.

— It lessened — Julie said, after observing the distance again.

— Then take that sensation that decreased... and bring it to the closer point.

She obeyed.

— Interesting... the four becomes three.

— And take that thing that still bothers... and send it to the far away point.

A few more seconds passed.

— Now bring it close. And do this: back and forth.

Julie's eyes began to move more fluidly.

— Now it's already a rocking motion — she said, surprised.

— You can move? And you haven't stopped walking? — Esly concluded with a smile. — That was just the doctor's way of making you stay still.

— Doctor's trick. That worked really well. Maybe too well. — Julie laughed.

— Then let's remove that "too well." Because you're no longer on that table. And you never stopped walking. You just stayed still at the time because you had to. Go ahead and explain all of this to her.

Julie nodded.

— Keep going back... as much as you want. Back and forth... — Esly guided the focus gently.

More silence. A tender silence.

— I'm almost sure it's nonsense — said Julie, then added: — But it was very serious, right?

— At the time, you did have to stay still. You just didn't need all that fear. That was the doctor's way to make you cooperate. Because there really was a risk. But how did you keep walking, jumping, playing? — the therapist asked challengingly. — That means you can play... even after cutting your tongue. And you can walk, even after a lumbar puncture. Yes or no?

— Yes.

— Does the little girl believe it?

— Now she believes. — Julie confirmed.

— The girl at the closer spot. Does she believe it?

Julie hesitated.

— Almost. I think she's a bit stubborn, right?

— She pouted at that doctor...

The therapist smiled and encouraged:

— Shall we say a few more things to that doctor? Go ahead, say something to him.

Julie was silent for a few seconds, then burst into laughter.

— Liked it, huh? Liked that! — the therapist confirmed, laughing along with Julie. — Got to tell the doctor a few hard truths, right?

— That's right. My mother came in. My mother defended me.

The therapist nodded tenderly.

— Look at the far away point — the therapist requested. — See how the little girl at the far point is doing. What do you see now?

— Far away, there's nothing anymore.

— Then bring that "nothing" to this point up close. Let's see what happens.

— It's the same as the previous little girl... afraid of being left alone...

— What could happen if she lets go?

— She could come back and be forgotten... and she'd be scared again. — Julie explained.

— But the younger girl already knows it's not like that and can explain to her: "Nothing's going anywhere."

— "Nothing's going anywhere." Does she need the pain to remember it?

Silence.

— Look... I think it's a belief that's been here for a long time, huh? — Julie observed. — But the four-year-old... she doesn't believe that anymore... And the six-year-old is anxious, but that means we finished hers well, right? Since she's talking about the ones...

— I don't know. You're the one who has to tell me.

Julie took a deep breath.

— I always feel it in my chest... like it's really the needle.

— And it's painful, right?

— Like a puncture in the chest — she added, hand near her left collarbone. — But it's right where the violin rests. That's where it is supported — she said, pointing to the instrument's position.

The therapist furrowed her brow.

— This six-year-old played the violin?

— No. Not yet. She played the keyboard. Didn't even dream of ever having a violin.

— Didn't know what it was.

— It was a tiny guitar. — Julie laughed, thinking of her six-year-old innocence.

— Tell me... how is the six-year-old? The one who had to endure the lumbar puncture.

— She's become just an image. Far away, distant.

— Take your gaze to the wall and check again. — Esly guided her once more.

Julie inhaled and looked.

— How is it there?

— It's like I feel that fear of movement in other points — Julie frowned. — But it's not there anymore. It's like that image connects to this moment. But it's not related. Yet I feel it in my body... it doesn't make sense.

— So, what is your body telling you with that?

— It's like it wants protection.

— Normal, right? — the therapist validated. — It feels attacked.

— Yeah. Like it could hide...

— Then go back and forth from the wall point to here, to the close point. Five, six, seven... ten seconds this way. Then that way.

A few more moments... Julie remained still.

— Wow! I even feel spasms in my hands. It's like a hiccup.

Another silence.

— It's no longer connected to that moment. — Julie affirmed confidently.

— It's become a photo from the past... And how is the six-year-old? Look at the wall... at the far point...

— There's nothing left.

— And here up close?

— It's all calm now.

— Are you following my pointer?

— Yes, there's nothing... I just think, like with the other girl, she needs some time. To leave that place... where she's understanding, settling in. But she knows she's done with it.

— Are you following my pointer? — Esly moved the pointer back to the limit of the wall.

Julie confirmed with a gesture and started laughing again, waving goodbye to the pointer.

— That's all folks! — she said, referencing the childhood cartoons, laughing playfully.

— Close your eyes. Let go of the point... you can open your eyes now. Tell me. What did you notice?

Julie took a deep breath.

— It calmed the child. All of the children.

— The whole tribe! Because there are still more in there... it wasn't just the cut wound.

— Yeah. But it gave that calming feeling. A really good sensation. It's like I'm feeling gravity differently, the weight in my body is different. The same feeling I had when I was preparing to go on stage. And it didn't matter if someone in neon green was in the audience, which can be very distracting. I went on. I had my center of gravity. It was distributed through my legs. I felt my whole body. And I knew what each arm had to do. And the music... it came. The music isn't here yet, but this bodily sensation... that I didn't remember... it's here already.

The therapist smiled with her.

— You're getting ready. There are you and your instrument. Nothing else.

— Exactly. — Julie agreed. — It's that connection... like a continuation of my body. Funny.

The weight of expectations and precision of technique had always been present. But she knew: the body responded differently when playing.

— Gravity can feel different... — she murmured, almost thinking aloud. — We assume another posture when we play.

The security of that core knowledge — firmly, silently built — was undeniable. Years of practice, countless hours of repetition. A mastery now seemingly dormant, but not lost.

—   Many   years   understanding   this   axis.   Like riding   a   bicycle...   You   learn   it   and   you   never   lose   it.

— Esly shared sincerely, knowing from experience what Julie meant.

— You sit down... and it all comes back. Brain, emotion... It's a direct connection, it leaves thought behind.

When playing, there's no room for lengthy thoughts. The movement requires lightness, speed, precision.

— The more you think, the more it interferes with the playing. — Julie concluded.

— The more you think, the slower it gets. The finger has to know what to do. The finger knows. Your violin is close by?

— Oh, I'm scared! — Julie exclaimed, eyes wide.

— No, just get it. Get the case. No need to play.

— It's here. — Julie had stood to retrieve it, still in the same room.

— No need to open it. Nothing, if you don't want to. — The therapist affirmed empathetically.

— I'll open it, yes. It's beautiful... and I love it so much... and I don't even look at it.

There was longing in that touch as she held it, the silent memory.

— Feeling nostalgic?

— Yes! It even has a name — Julie responded, animated — "Rô." An Anderson Rodrigues. I chose a Brazilian one. And he's beautiful!

She spoke with affection, familiarity, proudly showing the instrument.

— I even kept the same shoulder rest. The last one I bought, twenty years ago. I only changed the clasp.

The therapist then asked gently:

— When you look at it, what does it say to you?

Julie answered promptly:

193

— It's lighter than I thought... and maybe this can be done step by step. I don't need to start with Bach's E Major concerto. But it won't be Twinkle Twinkle Little Star either. — She laughed.

— Your fingers know much more than that — the therapist replied with a smile. — Even after twenty years. They know a lot. You can put it away now and close the case, if you like.

The memory was sensory.

— It's funny... like it had fallen asleep after a while. — Julie still referred to the instrument.

— It was asleep. "Beauty sleep." It just needed a kiss to wake up. — Esly answered.

— It will stay closer to me now. It can stay here, nearer. Right beside me. There is a time for everything.

— So... what are you taking home today?

Julie smiled:

Even I got emotional — Esly said. — I remembered when I reconnected with my paintbrushes. I realized... I don't have to paint a Picasso. The first ones won't be amazing. But they won't be Twinkle Twinkle Little Star either.

— They won't be — Julie laughed.

— But I can do something that satisfies my soul... because, in the end, Julie, you don't play for others. You play for your soul. — The therapist reinforced. — That's why there could be neon green shirt in the audience, and you wouldn't even see it. Because it wasn't for them. It was for you.

Julie smiled, touched.

— And you're healing — said the therapist, with a steady gaze. — You're integrating these wounds. Because the last one we haven't worked on yet was like, "Enough! I'm not doing this anymore." And now you can ask yourself... what kind of "no" is this? You have to be able to choose! If you want to play on the weekend, just for yourself... why not?

— Yeah, I don't have to stop walking, stop talking, stop playing...

— "I didn't stop walking. I didn't stop talking. I didn't stop playing. And I even learned a new instrument" — the therapist completed, speaking for Julie. — Close your eyes a little. See where you want to keep this hope inside you. This understanding...

Julie slowly closed her eyes.

— Ah! It's the butterfly hug, huh? — Julie said with a smile, eyes closed, positioning her arms, hands on her chest, like a butterfly hug. — That's the feeling. Right where it rests.

The therapist watched, very touched.

— Because it's sensory. Feeling the violin vibrate on your chest, in your head... with every different vibrato. The difference in the strings, the positions... And how it resonates! It's wonderful! — Julie delighted in the sensation, these old memories now flowing endlessly, making her body respond as if she were on an important stage.

Another silence. The therapist then spoke firmly: — This is yours forever now. Very beautiful, Julie.

— Thank you!

— Even if you never play again, you have this now. And maybe, because you have this, you can play. But you're not obliged to. And if you play, play whatever you want. Okay?

Julie nodded, smiling.

— Our time is up today — the therapist said. — You will still need to work on the hand injury. I'll let you work on that with someone else.

— Okay. Thank you!

— We already got off to a good start!

Julie laughed again.

Part 5

Brainspotting Sessions Z-Axis with the Resource Eye

Chapter 12

Rebeca's Three Children

Iprayed, I asked God... it was the pregnancy I had always dreamed of all my life. My husband and I waited a long time for this. — Rebeca began, and within seconds her eyes filled with tears, her voice trembling.

But when her daughter was born, the expected joy gave way to collapse.

— A series of sequential events happened. I had postpartum depression. It lasted almost two years. My mind wasn't working. I didn't return to normal after she was born.

She remembered a specific day, when her daughter was already nine months old, and she was holding her in her arms:

— I held her with joy. I thought, "Wow, how wonderful that I have a daughter." But it was much more exhausting than pleasurable... much more.

The birth had been traumatic.

— I had a lot of hemorrhaging. They handed me the baby, but I didn't want to hold her. I was worried I was going to die... I felt like she would slip out of my hands.

The hemorrhaging continued even after she was discharged from the hospital.

— Six days later, at home, I bled again. I went to the hospital. I had to receive a blood transfusion... two bags of blood.

As if that wasn't enough, her uterus got an infection soon afterwards.

— There was this huge chaos... I didn't even know what was really happening. I had to go back to the hospital, and face a curettage. I went without food for over a day. The milk didn't come in. I wanted to breastfeed, but at the same time, I didn't. I would say, "I don't like breastfeeding. I won't do it anymore."

Her husband tried to respect her decision.

— He said, "Okay. I'll go down and buy formula, we'll give it to her."

And she would collapse:

— "You're not going to do that! You'll take my daughter from me! You'll steal her!"

The cycle was insane:

— I gave breastfed in tears. Because I didn't want to, but I also didn't want her to die of hunger. It was twenty-four hours a day with my head in a mess.

Today, the little girl is six years old. The boy came next, three years younger.

— My pregnancy with my son was wonderful. The postpartum? Peaceful. I feel a much stronger connection with him than with her.

Silence. And then the phrase that hurt the most:

— It's as if I couldn't bond with her.

From the beginning, there had been distance. After the birth, Rebeca didn't want to hold Alice in her arms. Nor look at her too much. There was silent internal bleeding. She didn't know. She just felt her body was heavy. When the baby cried, she tried to get up—and fell.

— I would get up and faint. That's all. I just got up and I would faint.

Her husband would lift her from the floor. Others would pick up the child and place her in her mother's arms, because she couldn't reach the crib.

— That lasted about seven days, until they discovered the hemorrhaging. Then I went to the hospital.

Meanwhile, her daughter was left without her. She wasn't allowed into the hospital room. The baby went home; the mother stayed.

— One day the doctor said, "Bring the baby to be with her. If she stays away this long, when she's discharged, she won't want to hold her child."

During procedures with me, the child couldn't stay. But later, she would spend a few days in the mother's room. Returning home wasn't the end of it. She went back to the hospital. It was two endless months of coming and going, an unstable, broken rhythm, where no bond could really take hold.

— The first time we really spent time together was New Year's Eve.

The girl was born at the end of November. It took over a month before they were truly together at the same time and in the space.

Soon after, another hospitalization: mastitis, inflammation, infection, pain.

— I held the nurse's hand and said, "For goodness's sake, do something. I don't want to come back here. I can't take it anymore."

The desire to be a mother had always existed. But at that moment, motherhood felt like a punishment.

— My life became hell. If I could go back, I wouldn't have had her.

She spoke with guilt, but without hesitation. She knew what she was feeling.

— It wasn't that I didn't want to be a mother. It was because of what I was going through. Later came the other one... and if I could, I would have had more. But at that time, I thought it was the worst choice of my life. I cared for her because I knew I had to. But I didn't want to. Anyone else could do it. Anyone. As long as it wasn't me.

The therapist wondered out loud: how much of that was postpartum depression and how much was trauma?

— I don't know. I don't know what was depression and what was post-traumatic stress disorder.

The therapist responded firmly:

— It doesn't seem like it happened "out of nowhere." You nearly died several times. You have every reason for all of what you are describing.

And she remembered: two hemorrhages in two months, and the constant feeling that death was near.

— The doctor said, "We have no explanation for why this happened." And I thought, "It will happen again. I'm going to die."

She didn't want to leave. She didn't want to leave the hospital. At least there, she felt she had some chance.

— I would say, "If it happens again at home, I won't make it in time. I'm going to die."

But they wouldn't allow her to stay hospitalized indefinitely. The fear went with her wherever she went.

— I thought about it all the time. That I was going to die. That no one would save me. That I wouldn't be able to take care of her. That I would never enjoy anything again. That I was going to die.

In one episode, she hemorrhaged at home. Her husband drove to the hospital. Her mother sat in the back seat with her. The blood wouldn't stop. It stained the entire car.

— When we got close to the hospital, my mother started crying.

At that moment, a certainty settled in.

— I thought: "If she's crying… she already knows. I'm going to die."

Her mother cried without stopping, as if she had already given up. And Rebeca interpreted it as a confirmation of her imminent death. She was certain she wouldn't make it.

— At the same time, I thought I didn't want my daughter anymore... I thought: "If I die, who will take care of her?" And my mind... my mind never went back to the way it was before.

After the birth came the conflicts. Her marriage got really shaky. She yelled a lot.

— I would ask for a towel and he wouldn't bring it... then I'd scream. "If it weren't for God... and my husband's patience... I think my marriage wouldn't exist anymore.

Her mind couldn't keep up with the world around her.

The therapist asked her to rate her activation, from zero to ten. She answered without hesitation:

— Ten.

— And where do you feel it in your body?

— I don't know... I'm trembling. My chest... my arms are shaking. As if I were cold... but I'm not.

The therapist guided her to find her resource eye. She tried, adjusting her glasses, covering one eye, then the other, evaluating what she felt on each side. The left side seemed more intense.

— I think six, seven...

— And the other eye?

— Around nine.

She covered the more activated eye to look through the resource eye. The therapist guided her in finding the corresponding brainspot with the Inner Window with the resource eye—up, down, centered. Each change of angle brought a new sensation.

— More here... more in the middle... up... lower...

— And now, looking here... from zero to ten, how is it?

— Very bad.

— How bad is "very bad"?

— Nine.

The therapist asked her to look through the spot firmly, to the distance.

— And now?

— Six.

So the resource spot was the faraway and that is where they began to work. This was the entry point.

— Now think about your body. Where inside your body do you feel cam and safe?

She fixed her gaze on far away, on the resource point. The therapist invited her to stay there, allowing whatever came up, to come up.

And it did.

— It keeps going through my mind... that she was just an innocent child.

Silence.

— Now it keeps going through my head... they were innocent.

Another moment. Her voice broke.

— As if I were, too.

— And you were. — The psychologist affirmed.

She nodded slowly. Then she remembered something she had never said out loud:

— After she was born... I was very afraid that God would punish me. Take her away.

She became ill, and the fear came like a sentence. With each hospital visit, a prayer.

— I prayed... and asked God not to take her. — At that moment, Rebeca sobbed.

The therapist perceive she had touched something deep inside of her.

— And you needed to be punished for what? What did you do wrong?

— For everything.

And she went through her list, almost vomiting the words, without hesitation, as if reciting a memorized list of sins:

— For not wanting to breastfeed her, for not wanting to hold her when she was born. For not feeling joy when she arrived. For everything. For regretting having a child, for thinking it ruined my marriage.

The next memory came with image and sound.

— There was a time when the doctor ran a lab test and said: "The baby is fine. What about you?" That day, I couldn't stop crying. And it was just a throat infection. I just thought I was so grateful to God for not taking her. Many times, over almost seven years. Many. I remember some...

There were days when the idea seemed unbearable. She wondered if it wouldn't be better if she herself died.

— And then have someone else take care of her. Someone who could do better than me. — It wasn't just a vague idea. It was guilt repeating itself. — I kept making this huge mess... all the time.

The therapist responded with empathy:

— I got the impression that you were doing the best you could at that moment, handling what the situation required of you. Thank God you had people to help you, you had your mother, your husband, your faith.

— There were indeed a lot of people. — Rebeca agreed.

— Nurses, doctors...

— Oh, there really were a lot of people.

She remembered well the despair that took over when she arrived home with the baby from the hospital. The house was full, about fifteen people, all wanting to be a part, take photos, crowds every moment.

— Me giving her a bath... — she recounted — there about ten people in the room watching.

The presence of family multiplied: father-in-law, mother-in-law, her mother, her father, sister, brother-in-law. The room was packed.

The therapist, firmly, intervened:

— I'm going to start putting order in this situation. First step: Let's send everyone out of the room. Everyone goes to the living room.

She explained that one doesn't visit a new mother for at least a month, because she needs peace and quiet, to adjust, to learn how to do things. Especially a first-time mother, for whom everything was new and everything mattered.

— That's something I really wanted to have done back then. — Rebeca stated with conviction.

— We can't work, neither you nor I, with all these people in here. Send them away. Tell your husband to send your relatives to the living room, or out. "Later we'll show, later you show the baby, but give me some peace here."

The psychologist proposed:

— Who do you want to stay with you?

— Only Alice, my daughter!

— Tell your husband: "You and everyone else, go. Leave. Let me stay here quietly with her."

When people weren't around, everything felt a little lighter. The exhaustion was enormous. On top of that, there was the real fear of dying.

— I want to make you a proposal, — the psychologist said — if you agree. You can say no, no problem at all.

She suggested that they needed to speak to God for help in organizing everything:

— I'm not sure we can handle organizing this on our own. Because we need help. Shall we talk to Him?

She asked Rebeca to close her eyes for a few moments. She wanted her to imagine being the God she believes in—a role reversal. When she was ready, she could open her eyes. Then Esly began:

— I want to thank You, Lord, for coming here to talk with us. Because I'm troubled about a few things. Rebeca has been through so much, I don't even know everything. But You know, right? You know everything. You know what happened when her daughter was born. I want to tell You a few things she told me. Because I need to bring Your message back to her, as she believes deeply in You and in Your Word. I'm going to tell You some things You already know...

She said that, earlier in the session, Rebeca had confessed something difficult to say out loud: that she thought God would take her daughter away to punish her.

— Because she didn't behave well. Because she didn't know how to do things, didn't know how to take care of her. You need to explain to her, Lord... She was traumatized. You understand what it's like to nearly die. Her daughter was a blessing. But also a source of great pain at that moment. The possibility of dying was real, not just fear. Hemorrhage... You know how that is. But would You really do something like that to her? I don't have that impression of You. Jesus said that even when we, being imperfect, give good things to our children, how much more the Heavenly Father, right? That's the impression I have. But I could be mistaken. Because You are Rebeca's God... And sometimes perceptions differ... Can You explain if You would really do that to her?

Rebeca responded, in the role of God:

— I remember that Rebeca called my name all the time. I love her very much. She was unwell and kept calling out for Me. There was a day she said: — "If with God we go through all this, without God it would be hell itself."

Rebeca stayed silent as tears came quickly. The therapist added tenderly:

— And You were there. You didn't leave, didn't pack up and disappear.

The emotion grew. Rebeca's face was covered with tears.

— She fought to love her daughter the whole time. — Rebeca continued, still speaking as God.

— She told me that too. — The therapist agreed, making a subtle gesture toward her heart.

207

— And there's more, Lord. You see the heart, things I cannot see. You know her intention. Her desire. And her impossibility. Tell me... Would You really have punished her for all this?

The answer came, clear and firm.

— No. I was trying to take care of her and her daughter. She had a lot to learn. — Rebeca still spoke in the role of God.

— A tough way to learn, huh, God. — the psychologist said, empathetic.

With her eyes still fixed on the point, Rebeca responded:

— But she did. — Speaking of herself. The silence afterward was almost reverent.

— She managed because You were there too. You cared, protected... and kept her from dying — the therapist completed. — Because when we do something truly wrong, we do one of two things: we either punish ourselves... or forgive ourselves. But I didn't see that Rebeca did anything wrong.

— The problem isn't what she did. It's the things she can't go back and relive... hold her daughter, go for a walk. — The phrase came heavy, as if chewing each syllable.

— Ah, but You own time. You own time! — The therapist waited, as if expecting an answer. — She can! But first... first she has to lose the fear that You'll take her daughter away. I want to know if You would do that.

— No. No. — Rebeca answered, a gentle urgency in her voice.

— You will let her keep her daughter?

— Yes. Now and later on, too. When she grows up, she will always be with her.

— She's not going away? No plan of Yours for that?

Rebeca shook her head.

— Then I can tell Rebeca to stay calm? That this won't happen?

She waited. Rebeca still shook her head.

— Then this is a message. What other message do You want me to give her?

Rebeca still cried:

— I love both of them. And I see her trying very hard. — A faint smile appeared. — Trying is already a big deal.

— Will You honor all the effort she's making? — The therapist confirmed.

— Yes. — Rebeca answered confidently.

— Do You have advice for me? I'm trying to help her with all this. Do You have any advice on what I can do to help her? Because she really wants to be closer to her daughter. She regrets that things weren't different. But she did her best. She gave her the best she had to give at the time. Even what she didn't have... she gave. But, You know human things. We live in time. We have a beginning, middle, and end. You don't have those, but we do. — The therapist asked reverently: — Do You have advice for me, on how I can help her?

— Let her go back and do what she didn't do.

— Agreed. — She nodded in agreement.

And, lightly, as if ending a ritual:

— I want to thank You, Lord, for coming here and talking with us. And giving me this good advice. Now I will bring these messages back to her. I am very grateful. Thank You. — Esly paused for a moment — Now, Rebeca, close your eyes. Stop being "God" and go back to being Rebeca. Let me know when you're back.

She waited.

— I'm here. — Rebeca answered.

The therapist closed her own eyes briefly, as if she had really returned from an intimate conversation. Then she looked at Rebeca gently.

— Rebeca, I went to have a talk with God. I spoke with Him where He lives, you know? — the therapist began softly. — He told me some things, gave me important messages. First: this fear that God will take your daughter to punish you... He never thought that. There was never a plan for punishment.

Rebeca frowned, unsure.

— I still think about it — she admitted. — He already took my husband's brother... and if He takes her later, when she grows up?

— But as a punishment?

— No, it was an accident.

— That was an accident, not a punishment — the therapist assured. — Accidents happen, but they're different. Punishment would mean intention. And, from what I heard from Him, there's no such intention. I want to know if you really believe that God will punish you for all that happened with you and your daughter?

Rebeca shook her head.

— Really gone? Take a deep breath. Once more. Breathe into your belly.

— I feel relieved not having to worry about that anymore.

— Don't worry anymore, that wasn't a sin. You didn't do anything that deserved punishment. And He wouldn't take her from you. She was an answer to your prayer, right? You asked God for her, asked to become pregnant and have a daughter.

Rebeca was still crying, nodding her head.

— Now close your eyes for a moment, Re. Go inside, to your body resource spot, and see if you can now believe that God will not take your daughter as punishment.

— I believe! — Her voice was strong, yet still trembling, from real emotion.

— You can open your eyes and return to the pointer, the far away spot. How does it feel now?

— Calmer, much calmer. It's lighter to be her mother without thinking she's going to die.

— She's not going to die. And more, Rebeca isn't going to die either. I want you to tell the Rebeca inside you, the one who had this daughter: "Look, we didn't die and we're not going to die. We are here as proof."

Rebeca nodded in agreement and repeated as instructed.

— God wants to say that He recognized and greatly admired your effort. The fact that you tried to do things right, even when you couldn't manage. There was no bad intention on His part. No malice. Just limitations... Limitations of that moment. Very big ones. That's why the reactions were so intense. — Esly took a breath and added: — But God understood this. He wants to say that He admires you very much. He appreciated, really appreciated your efforts. He saw that you were trying really hard. Trying to get it right. But at that time... everything got confusing. Now breathe. Receive this message from Him.

Tears streamed down her face, rivalling any waterfall. Her voice trembled:

— I feel better. — Rebeca said calmly, crying, but with a faint smile.

— Sometimes we don't realize it, but He stands there and applauds us. For that, we have a "cloud of witnesses." Everyone was clapping and rejoicing.

— Yes...

The therapist brought another insight:

— And He gave me some advice for you. He said to go back to that memory and redo it. — She paused. — Are you willing?

Rebeca nodded.

— Then return your gaze to the pointer. What is the level now?

— Four.

— Okay. And with whom do you want to redo this pathway?

— Alone with God.

— You, alone with God? Alright. Can I follow, just a little bit, from afar?

211

— Yes. I was already saying that you'd go along anyway. I said it was just me and God because I didn't want my husband or anyone else there. Just us.

— Then let's go, right? Because, since God gave me this advice... He's coming with us. So, let's go. To the hospital. Your baby was born...

— What I wanted most was to hold her.

— Then let's hold her. Here she comes...

A faint smile appeared amid the tears.

— She was so beautiful. — Rebeca was deeply moved.

— There's nothing like it in the world, right? I'll tell you something... There's only one thing more beautiful than giving birth... It's seeing your daughter give birth. And you'll see that, because you have a daughter.

Rebeca nodded, breathing steadily while wiping her face. The therapist continued:

— Let's put this aside for a moment. The doctors are nearby. Many things are happening, and we need to do some procedures so you can enjoy your daughter more. Okay? You have a hemorrhage. Your body had some problems. Now I want you to imagine the solution. The remedy. I don't know if it's a kind of Holy Spirit cauterization, or some medicine, an ointment, something they do there. Imagine something to stop the bleeding, so it won't come back. God will show you because He's with us.

— Esly, something very important came to me right now. I want it to be like a little powder. For us to sprinkle it there, a forgiveness powder. Because my uterus wasn't able to hold the other baby before her and I had the miscarriage.

— Okay. Then let's pause. Let's open another chapter. Let's put this aside for a moment. It will stay gently in a kind of "heavenly crock pot", resolving on its own while we deal with this other thing here.

The therapist kept the pointer steady on the resource point, giving Rebeca space to access the memory that was surfacing—the first positive pregnancy result that was lost.

— I had a hemorrhage a year before Alice was born — she began, her voice still broken. — I didn't even know I was pregnant. I found out while I was bleeding. My friends from grad school said I looked pregnant, and I knew I wasn't, because I was bleeding. But I took a home test. It was positive, but the doctor said it was an ectopic pregnancy... They had to open my abdomen two days after I found out I was pregnant — she continued, shoulders hunched as if still feeling the scalpel. — They removed the entire tube. I went a year without wearing jeans, thinking the scar hurt. It hurt because it was my loss. I was very frightened because they had to open my abdomen. Later, the two other children were born naturally, but everyone said, "You already have the scar, do a C-section" and I always said no one will ever open my belly again.

Rebeca could barely speak.

— I begged God to move the embryo to the uterus, but it stayed where it shouldn't, in the tube. I asked God to move it so I could carry my baby. But that's not how it works. It felt it was like a punishment.

— A body navigational error, not a punishment. The baby didn't where it should have gone. — corrected the therapist.

Rebeca took a deep breath before continuing:

— I was in pain for a week before they removed it. It was the same with Alice... When I had her, I was in pain for a week. The baby stayed inside for a week, not knowing what it was, until the day it was removed.

She paused longer.

— It was horrible to have it removed.

The therapist gently suggested:

— So, shall we remove it in another way? — Her tone carried support. — We know that a baby like this will indeed go into God's presence.

Rebeca murmured, surprised at what she had just heard:

— I had never thought of that.

— There are special angels who come to take them — the therapist added, letting the image slowly take shape. — And in the Christian belief, you will see this baby again, you will meet the baby. You don't even know if it's a boy or a girl, but you will meet him or her.

Esly allowed the silence to do its work, then guided tenderly:

— Imagine that an angel is coming to get the baby. But before taking them, you can speak to your baby. You can speak to God. You can speak to the angel. You can speak to yourself, in your imagination. You don't even need to speak out loud if you don't want to.

The invitation was clear, gentle:

— But let's meet this baby. Let's tell him or her how much you love it. How much you wanted it. And that you regret it's not the right moment. That it's not going to happen this way. That you will entrust the baby to the Lord's care. And that someone very perfect will take care of it until you can get there.

Esly asked respectfully:

— What do you think? Does that feel right? You'll need to do it your way.

— Yes — Rebeca replied, with a gentle smile.

— Then, look at that spot and let's do that.

Silence. She kept her eyes fixed on the brainspot.

After a few moments, she spoke tenderly:

— It's tiny, in God's hand. With God's big hand... and my baby's little hand. He's safe. — Tears flowed abundantly, inevitable.

The therapist mirrored her sensitivity:

— That's it. Breathe deeply again. Is that okay?

— It's much better knowing he's there.

— Ah, that's wonderful! He's being cared for. He's waiting for you.

The therapist then directed Rebeca:

— Now, I want you to speak to your body.

She continued, intertwining faith and physiology:

— I don't know if you believe this way or not, but in the Christian doctrine, it says Jesus bled. He paid the price, on the cross. I think you need to tell your body that Jesus bled so your body doesn't have to do it. He told you to stop bleeding. You don't need that. The baby is already cared for. If you want to cry, cry through your eyes. But don't cry through your uterus. Cry through your eyes. That's the right place to cry.

She added with sweetness and firmness:

— That's enough for this baby who implanted in the wrong place. But you don't need to keep bleeding for it. Talk to your body. Your body is very traumatized. The body doesn't like to be opened. Never. No body does. God made the skin so things outside stay on the outside, and things inside, stay inside. However, sometimes it has to be opened, right? Yours had to be opened so you wouldn't die. Explain to your body what happened — the therapist said. — Explain for it to be at peace. So your body can have the next child.

Rebeca nodded.

— Because this won't lead to bleeding again — the therapist added. — Resolve all this with your body first.

Silence. Time for processing. Rebeca admitted:

— The baby was impatient, like me, you know? He implanted in the wrong place. — She smiled subtly, as if sharing a secret gracefully — Why choose to implant before reaching the right place? A little impatient... It's all okay now.

— Missed one of the tubes, but there's the other one, right?

— Right. The other works very well. I had two more children.

The therapist continued guiding:

— And now, yes, sprinkle a little powder, apply a little ointment... Calm your body, calm your uterus, calm your belly... And breathe once more. Open your chest and breathe.

Another moment of silence followed, then she said:

— I'll tell you something else I was told... is that okay? I don't know if it's exactly like this... but I was told. In heaven, when we arrive... there's only one thing from Earth: the scars of Jesus on His hands, feet, and chest...

Her voice was calm, loving.

— They say He has them because they represent the scars of victory. Of what He overcame. What He conquered.

She then proposed:

— I want you to look at your scar and say: "This is my victory scar, what I overcame. For what I achieved. I had a great loss. But I didn't die. And I still had two more children."

Rebeca breathed deeply.

— No need for more scars — the therapist added, returning focus — Now, go to the pointer. Keep looking. Work it out with your body.

A moment. One breath.

— We did it — Rebeca said, as if stating something already known.

— We managed to overcome this. And you still had two more children. And there's a little third one there... the first, actually, right? So cute.

Silence.

— I still have all three, right? — Rebeca said, with deep affection.

The therapist nodded:

— Yes. Three... So now, when you think about this first experience, this little baby... everything you lost and lived through... How do you rate it now, zero to ten?

— Zero — Rebeca answered without hesitation. About the little baby I lost, zero.

The therapist responded with warmth:

— It's not the baby you lost. It's the baby you entrusted. God adopted it and will always take care of it. Right?

Rebeca nodded, moved.

— Catholics speak a lot about the Holy Family... I find it so beautiful. That the Holy Family will take care of the baby. It's a whole family up there, I imagine. And a mother won't be missing to take care of him. Nor a father... Angels... He will grow in God's ways. And you'll keep him in your heart forever. Mothers never forget. That's why God says that even if a mother could forget a child, He doesn't forget us. And that our names are written on the palms of His hands. — Her voice lowered even more: — Just like your child's name is written in your hear, right? — asked the therapist.

— It is.

— Later, when you feel longing for that baby, you can say: "Wait a little longer. I'm coming. At the right time, I'm coming." And you put it back into your heart.

Another silence.

— Can we leave this piece here? [Pause.] Then keep it in the heavenly file. And let's return to the other matter we're still unpacking...

— Now it seems to hurt much.

— And it is much less, now that you can cry through the eyes— said the therapist, tenderly — That's the proper way to cry.

Rebeca breathed more freely.

— Now we've managed to find a way to do this cauterization so there's no need for so much hemorrhaging

— I think now it's just a matter of letting a natural process happen. A normal postpartum. The uterus cleans itself, does everything properly. — Rebeca spoke, gradually forming the image in her mind.

— Her first bath was much calmer now — said Rebeca, smiling.

— Even better because it's just you, right? — the therapist joked.

— Sleeping with her is more enjoyable. Because it doesn't hurt when she touches me. Breastfeeding her is wonderful.

— Wonderful!

— Alice nursed until she was three years and five months.

The therapist smiled.

— So, you overcame all this? Even the mastitis?

— Even the mastitis — confirmed Rebeca.

— You are so strong! Amazing!

— It's all okay. She will stay here with me. I can enjoy her. And live my life with her. Without worrying that she will die at some point. It's so much better this way!

— And you're no longer bleeding. You've had children the normally way now.

Rebeca agreed with a slight gesture.

— No punishment! Now look at Alice again. Everything that happened... from zero to ten, how is it now?

— Zero — Rebeca answered firmly. — I imagine her in my arms all the time — she added. — It's easier to hold her now because nothing hurts. Not my heart. Not my belly. Not anything. It's easier to hold her now.

— Then watch her grow — the therapist suggested. — She's one... Two... Three... Up to today. See yourself hugging, hugging... embracing her...

— She's so big today — said Rebeca, laughing. — And still clingy. She loves hugs. Loves kisses. She really enjoys being held. She's amazing. — Then, with a calmer, deeper voice, Rebeca admitted: — I'm not afraid of losing her anymore.

— That's because "perfect love casts out fear." You're connecting with the love you have for her. And letting go. Freeing yourself from the fear of dying. That's what was blocking you.

Silence.

— Is that okay? — asked the therapist.

— It's perfect.

— Think for a moment... take a deep breath. See what you want to take home.

— I want her, to hold her now.

— Absolutely.

— I don't even know if she's awake yet. It's all okay.

The therapist suggested:

— Don't you think it's good to give thanks to God? He is near, seeing and hearing.

— Thank you so much, Lord! Thank you, because I could only get here because You were with me. I think of You doing all this for me, with me... it has to be Your work. I couldn't stand to be away from my daughter my whole life. Thank you, Esly. I really want to thank you.

The therapist followed gently:

— I thank you. Close your eyes. Release the point. Take off your glasses and let's dry your face.

Rebeca obeyed silently. In the next moment, her voice came low, choked with emotion:

— I have an immense feeling of gratitude.

She paused. Her chest rose and fell slowly.

— For the times when, in fact, we think we're alone... — said Rebeca — and the truth is I was carried in someone's arms.

— Yes. He carried you in His arms — confirmed the therapist.

— He carried me. I feel relieved. It's like a weight has been lifted off my back.

— Let me tell you something... — said the therapist calmly. — I think God doesn't need time. But we operate in time. — That's why the pain comes back, because there's a part of our brain where these things are always happening. Now we've managed to take it from that place and put it in the Past File. In a good place. Now you can do with it as you wish.

A sweet silence passed between them.

— And now you have a very beautiful story. — Esly smiled as she spoke. — I hope it becomes even more beautiful as Alice grows up. It's a beautiful story of how you fought to keep her and stay with her.

Rebeca nodded.

— You didn't let go, you didn't give up. In the midst of all the suffering... you held on.

— Yes — Rebeca confirmed.

— That is called love.

She took a deep breath, her eyes still wet.

— Thank you, Esly.

— Thank you for your trust.

And outside, an unexpected sound was heard. It was a rooster crowing behind Rebeca.

— Look, the rooster is crowing! It's a new day — said the therapist, laughing.

— It's because he lives in the city. At night there's light, he gets a little off schedule. — Rebeca explained, laughing. — Thank you again, it's a new beginning.

— New day, new beginning — confirmed Esly.

Epilogue

I hope you have enjoyed this journey through the inner lives of our clients as much as I have been touched and moved by what Brainspotting can do. Each session was 60-90 minutes long, and even in front of other colleagues, you can see how powerful changes can be effected in such a short amount of time.

Hopefully, these stories will encourage you to try Brainspotting as you seek your healing journey, and to my Brainspotting colleagues, perhaps you saw how Psychodrama methodology can be integrated with the Brainspotting techniques we teach and use.

Although this is a first casebook of Brainspotting sessions, it is my sincere desire that it will not be the last, and that others will be challenged to share their stories as we expand the possibilities of healing worldwide.

Once again, thanks to David Grand for having the courage to follow his instinct and inspiration, and developed this revolutionary approach. To all the unnamed colleagues who allowed us to share their stories, you have given others an amazing gift. And to Bianca, thank you for helping me to tell these stories in a way that others can appreciate and learn from them.

See you in the next book!

Esly Carvalho
Author

Glossary

- **Activation**: increase in emotional, bodily, or cognitive intensity related to the therapeutic topic.
- **Brainspot**: a specific eye position associated with subcortical responses relevant to the emotional content.
- **X/Y/Z Axis**: visual coordinates used to locate brainspots; the Z-axis refers to depth and influences processing intensity
- **Outside Window**: brainspots discovered by observing reflexive responses (blinks, tremors, breathing).
- **Inside Window**: brainspots discovered through the client's subjective perception, without using a pointer.
- **Rolling Spotting**: continuous lateral eye movement until an activation point emerges, which may or may not involve a pointer.
- **Gazespotting**: observation of natural eye fixation to locate the brainspot.
- **One-Eyed Brainspotting**: when the client covers one eye to find the resource eye and the activation eye.
- **Dual Attunement**: relational and neurobiological attunement between therapist and client, sustained by attentive presence (GRAND, 2013).
- **SUDS**: Subjective Units of Distress Scale, ranging from 0 to 10, in Brainspotting used to assess level of activation at a given moment. A score of 0 represents no activation, while 10 indicates the maximum level of activation.
- **Convergence Therapy**: method of vagus nerve activation via the Z-axis, used in the One-Eye/Three-Dimensional BSP modality (GRAND, 2013).

References

1. Books

BAUMANN, Monika. *Brainspotting with children and adolescents: an attuned therapy*. Viena: Independently published, 2018.

GRAND, David. *Brainspotting: the revolutionary new therapy for rapid and effective change*. Boulder, CO: Sounds True, 2013.

GRAND, David; GLICK, Alan. *This is your brain on sports: beating blocks, slumps and performance anxiety for good!*. New York: Dog Ear Publishing, 2016.

GRIXTI, Mark. *Brainspotting with young people: an adventure into the mind*. London: Matador, 2015.

WOLFRUM, Gerhard (org.). *The power of Brainspotting: an international anthology*. 1. ed. [S.l.]: Self-published, 2018.

ZACZYK, Christian. *Guérir des traumatismes psychiques avec le Brainspotting*. Paris: Odile Jacob, 2019.

2. Articles and Book Chapters

GRAND, David. *Brainspotting overview*. 2015.
Available at: https://www.emdrandpsychotherapy.com/wp-content/uploads/delightful-downloads/2015/04/david-grand-brainspotting.pdf. Retrieved: 12 July 2025.

ROSS, Cynthia; COHEN, David. *Brainspotting: a new brain-based psychotherapy approach*. Ross & Cohen Psychotherapy, 2017.
Available at: https://www.ross-cohen.com/brainspotting-article.
Retrieved: 12 July 2025.

3. Institutional Online Sources

BRAINSPOTTING INTERNATIONAL. *About Brainspotting*. 2024.
Available at: https://brainspotting.com/about-brainspotting.
Retrieved: 12 July 2025.

MIDWEST BRAINSPOTTING INSTITUTE. *Recommended reading list.* Available at: https://midwestbrainspottinginstitute.org/resources/. Retrieved: 12 July 2025.

THERAPLATFORM. *What is Brainspotting and how does it work? -* BLANCHFIELD, Theodora. Verywell Mind, 2023. Available at: https://www.verywellmind.com/brainspotting-therapy-definition-techniques-and-efficacy-5213947. Retrieved: 12 July 2025.

WORKS COUNSELING CENTER. *What is Brainspotting?*. 2022. Available at: https://workscounselingcenter.com/brainspotting/. Retrieved: 12 July 2025.

WIKIPEDIA. *Brainspotting*. 2025. Available at: https://en.wikipedia.org/wiki/Brainspotting. Retrieved: 12 July 2025.

About Esly Carvalho, Ph.D., T.E.P.

Esly Carvalho has a long international career in psychotherapy and training. TraumaClinic was founded by her to offer courses on trauma teaching and training, now in many countries and languages. She is a trainer of EMDR, Psychodrama and Brainspotting, as well an author of books on these topics. Presently she has begun using her artistic talent in combination with her therapeutic workbooks.

Works for sale:
https://www.redbubble.com/people/BrazilianOak

Other books, articles and courses:
www.traumaclinicinternational.com

About Bianca Breus Bassi

Clinical Psychologist with 13 years of experience, specializing in the application of neuroscience to therapy. Neuropsychologist certified by CBI of Miami, trained in EMDR and Brainspotting by TraumaClinic — approaches focused on trauma treatment and access to deep emotional processes. Currently pursuing a Master's degree in Neuroscience, Psychology, and Human Behavior. Founder of Compor Psicologia, where she develops lectures and programs dedicated to promoting mental health in corporate environments.

Contact:
Instagram
@biancabassi.psi
@comporpsicologia

www.comporpsi.com.br

www.ingramcontent.com/pod-product-compliance
Lightning Source LLC
Chambersburg PA
CBHW052127270326
41930CB00012B/2787